EVERYDAY HOLINESS

EVERYDAY HOLINESS

A GUIDE TO LIVING HERE AND GETTING TO ETERNITY

Carolyn Humphreys

Foreword by
James Kubicki

WIPF & STOCK · Eugene, Oregon

EVERYDAY HOLINESS
A Guide to Living Here and Getting to Eternity

Copyright © 2018 Carolyn Humphreys. All rights reserved. Except for brief quotations in critical publications or reviews, no part of this book may be reproduced in any manner without prior written permission from the publisher. Write: Permissions, Wipf and Stock Publishers, 199 W. 8th Ave., Suite 3, Eugene, OR 97401.

Wipf & Stock
An Imprint of Wipf and Stock Publishers
199 W. 8th Ave., Suite 3
Eugene, OR 97401

www.wipfandstock.com

PAPERBACK ISBN: 978-1-5326-4304-0
HARDCOVER ISBN: 978-1-5326-4305-7
EBOOK ISBN: 978-1-5326-4306-4

Manufactured in the U.S.A.

Heart of Jesus, Fountain of life and holiness

Heart of Jesus, Delight of all the saints

Contents

Acknowledgments | ix
Foreword | xi

Holiness: Our True Identity | 1
Faith: The Eternity Connection | 14
Hope: Evergreen | 26
Love: That Which Makes the World Go Round | 41
Discipleship: Following Jesus | 53
Prayer: Our Privilege and Our Gift | 66
Work: To Serve with Dignity | 79
Suffering: Grace Unexpected | 91
Perseverance: Like a Turtle on the Trail | 106
Joy: Inside a Christian Heart | 124
Eucharistia: Holy Adoration | 136
Eucharistia: Holy Communion | 148
Mystery: The Ineffability of God | 160
Gratitude: A Hymn from the Heart | 174

Bibliography | 185

Acknowledgments

My sincere thank you is graciously given to the following people. They have helped bring this book to reality by their clarifying advice, helpful suggestions, erudite observations, wise counsel, and laudable holiness: Father James Kubicki, SJ, Peggy Normandin, Father Christopher Troxell, Debi Hoppe, Anthony Farao, Barbara Harrend, and Ida Rubin.

Foreword

EVERY SO OFTEN I talk to people about being saints. Often the response is: "Not me. I'm no saint. I'll never be a saint." My response is: "Well, you better get to work because in the end there will be only two options: if you're not a saint, the alternative is pretty hot!"

We are all saints-in-the-making. To be a saint is our purpose and our ultimate goal in life. Jesus said, "Be holy as your heavenly Father is holy." He wouldn't command us to do something impossible. He called us all to holiness because we are made for union with the All-Holy One—God.

Pope John Paul II made it clear that holiness is not optional in the life of a Christian. He wrote: "I have no hesitation in saying that all pastoral initiatives must be set in relation to *holiness* (*Novo Millennio Ineunte*, n.30, emphasis in the original). He went on to say that "the universal call to holiness" was a major theme of the Second Vatican Council. "As the Council itself explained, this ideal of perfection must not be misunderstood as if it involved some kind of extraordinary existence, possible only for a few 'uncommon heroes' of holiness. . . .The time has come to re-propose wholeheartedly to everyone this *high standard of ordinary Christian living*: the whole life of the Christian community and of Christian families must lead in this direction" (*NMI* n.31).

If holiness is not for the few but for everyone, how does one become holy? Pope John Paul wrote that "the paths to holiness are personal and call for a genuine '*training in holiness*,' adapted to people's needs. This training must integrate the resources offered to everyone with both the traditional forms of individual and group assistance, as well as the more recent forms of support offered in associations and movements recognized by the Church. This training in holiness calls for a Christian life distinguished above all in *the art of prayer*" (*NMI* nn.31–32).

Training in holiness through the art of prayer is what Carolyn Humphreys offers in her book *Everyday Holiness*. With stories, wise sayings of

FOREWORD

the saints, poetry, lyrics, and her own reflections, Carolyn opens a treasure house for prayer, both traditional and new. Carolyn has done us a great service in bringing many resources together in an engaging and thorough way. She covers numerous aspects of holiness, including the theological virtues; everyday moments of work, prayer, and suffering; and the Eucharist, which, according to the Second Vatican Council, is "the source and summit of the Christian life."

Everyday Holiness reminds us that growth in holiness by going deeper in our prayer life is not optional. According to Pope John Paul II, "it would be wrong to think that ordinary Christians can be content with a shallow prayer that is unable to fill their whole life. Especially in the face of the many trials to which today's world subjects faith, they would be not only mediocre Christians but 'Christians at risk'" (*NMI* n.34). Life with its many challenges to faith is difficult enough, but in the "spiritual desert" of contemporary life, as Pope Benedict described it, we are at risk if we do not go deeper. At risk of what? We risk nothing less than losing our way through this life and into the next.

The New Evangelization has emerged as the antidote to the spiritual diseases of our time. What is proposed is not a "new gospel" but the gospel which is ever-new because it is given flesh by each new generation. Ultimately the best witness to the Gospel of Jesus Christ is the life of a holy Christian. True holiness is joyful. Holiness attracts others to the faith more effectively than anything else. But true holiness is only possible through prayer and the interior transformation that prayer brings about.

With *Everyday Holiness* Carolyn has made a practical contribution to the New Evangelization. Her book will make reflective readers discontent "with a shallow prayer that is unable to fill their whole life." *Everyday Holiness* inspires a desire for holiness which is ultimately the wholeness of a good life, a life in which daily prayer and action lead to the happiness for which God created each of us.

Everyday Holiness is a book to be read slowly and savored. Filled with both inspiration and practical advice, it can help both beginners in prayer and seasoned contemplatives go deeper in their spiritual lives.

Father James Kubicki, SJ
National Director
Apostleship of Prayer 2003–2017
Currently Director of St Francis Mission,
Rosebud Reservation, South Dakota

Holiness: Our True Identity

He was handsome, fun loving, courageous and engaging, an athlete and an outdoorsman. A popular picture of him as a young adult reveals the strong young man wearing mountain climbing gear, leaning on a long ice axe, with one foot resting sturdily on a rock. He wrote to a friend: "With every passing day I fall madly in love with the mountains, their fascination attracts me." Born into a prominent Italian family, he distinguished himself as a member of the Alpine Club and conquered several of Italy's highest peaks. He relished the challenge of testing his physical limits, but always had time to help his fellow hikers. He slowed down to walk with them on their mountain hikes and helped to carry their supplies. A month before his death, he climbed a high peak with friends. He later wrote at the bottom of a photo of that ascent: "Toward the top." This short phrase symbolized his way of life. Pier Giorgio Frassati always sought out challenges that carried him beyond himself to become the best he could be. He incorporated prayer and meditation into his daily life and mountain treks. He lived out his Catholic faith with fervent devotion and became a member of the Lay Dominicans. He spoke out on political issues, rejoiced in his love for music and art, and cared for the sick and the poor. On July 4, 1925, Pier Giorgio Frassati died from polio at age twenty-four. Today, young adult Catholics around the world perpetuate Pier's beautiful spirit of service by sponsoring hikes, service projects, and prayer gatherings in his honor. John Paul II beatified him on May 20, 1990.

Pier Giorgio demonstrates that a true Catholic Christian spiritual journey is a noble adventure. His legacy beckons all people of God and pilgrims of faith, to climb the rugged mountain of holiness. What does this mean? Mysterious and obscure in the modern world, holiness begins with perceiving the whole reality of life within the reality of God's love for us. It is not a topic for mere theological speculation, but rather a conviction to be lived. We live it through our individual uniqueness and our Catholic response to the various circumstances in our lives.

At first, the desire for holiness may be an unrecognized yearning, a searching for truth or a striving to be good. We experience a nameless hunger for something more than the world has to offer: The recognition of holiness is revealed when we discover that our only destiny is God, the way to God is Christ, and Christ is our ultimate holiness. The erudite Edith Stein offers insight about this nameless hunger: "God is truth. All who seek truth seek God whether this is clear to them or not."

The call to holiness can astound us. Who me? You have to be kidding! Nevertheless, there is a longing for God, whether we are consciously aware of it or not. Carl Jung said, "Bidden or not bidden, God is present." This longing becomes more prominent when worldly pursuits disappoint, or when persons or things let us down. We wonder, "Is that all there is?" If we truthfully answer this question, our longing for God takes us from the many detours promising instant happiness to the singular direction of eternal true joy. If we fail to find an attraction to God, it is not because God has failed to provide it. It is due to our shortsightedness, a failure to look beyond immediate circumstances to God's broader plan. It is easy to believe that security and happiness exist apart from God. But, in the long run, don't we find that many of the things we chase after are either elusive or unsatisfying? Pier Giorgio found the importance of God and lived this greatest discovery. He challenges us to do the same.

The Sun Begins to Rise

Holiness makes its first quiet dawn into a new day with the realization that there is something more to life than career, success, social status, physical pleasures, material comforts or other worldly gains. A new beginning, a different orientation to life, begins to shine. Something inexplicable nags at our subconscious. Something deeper, more satisfying than what the world offers. Our curiosity is piqued. We begin to seek satisfaction in nature and service, rather than in self-serving pursuits. One does not immediately recognize the truth that true happiness cannot be found apart from God, but the early light of dawn will begin to illuminate that fact. True authenticity is only found in God. God loves each individual more than anyone else possibly could. He desires what is best for us, and by far the best for us is to grow in holiness.

Holiness: Our True Identity

The following story shows how nature revealed a remarkable scene that changed a person's life:

> There was a man who lived on the Great Blasker island off the coast of Kerry, Ireland, who worked from dawn to dusk every day of the week. He owned a small flock of sheep. He was short of help, and his family being young, he had no time to check his sheep except on Sundays. So, instead of going across to the mainland to attend Mass with the other islanders, he would take his stick and his dog and go up the hill to check on his sheep. It wasn't that he had no faith.... It was just that he was a stubborn man who always did what suited himself.
>
> His wife often tried to get him to change his ways. She told him that he was not setting a good example for his children. Why couldn't he check on his sheep after returning from Mass, as his neighbors did? But he ignored her.
>
> One Sunday, when all the islanders had gone to Dunquin to Mass, he went up the hill as usual. Since the wind was from the south, he went to the north side of the island, expecting to find the sheep there. But there wasn't a sheep to be found. Puzzled, he then went to the south side, and to his surprise found the sheep there. He was amazed to see them gathered into one spot, a marvelous beam of light shining down on them through a break in the clouds.
>
> This simple scene made a deep impression on him. The result was that the following Sunday, he was the first to arrive on the pier to get the boat to Dunquin for Mass. And he never again missed Mass on a Sunday.[1]

Living holiness is unique, affects every part of a person, and influences one's outlook on life. An individual builds a friendship with God through prayer, the teachings and traditions of religion, in sacraments and sacramentals, worship and praise, rites and rituals, study, labor, leisure, rest, saint watching and works of service. Friendship with God is noticeable in everything a person does. The beauty of a holy life is the most powerful influence in this world. Someone said sanctity is the highest level of maturity.

The journey to holiness is usually a slow and steady process, with few, if any, extraordinary mystical events. It does not take place outside, above or alongside other areas of life. It is the very essence of one's being, similar to the tranquility of a home where the soul thrives and the Triune God dwells. The author of *The Cloud of Unknowing* encourages: "If you wish to

---

1. Flor McCarthy, SDB, "Without a Vision the People Perish," *Spirituality*, July/August 2006.

keep growing you must nourish in your heart the lively longing for God. Though this loving desire is certainly God's gift, it is up to you to nurture it." Jesus alone satisfies the deep yearnings of the heart. The quest for Jesus should never end. Often an individual finds him, and then loses him only to find him again at a deeper, more intimate level. That very process leads to holiness.

The spiritual journey does not elevate a person above humanity or distinguish him as a singularly sacred being. Of course, there are always a few "bright light" saints who radiate God's goodness for the world to see, but most Christians are meant to be little flames of light, shining the love of Christ throughout daily routines, neither being oracles of wisdom nor fountains of advice. However, when a Christian has the opportunity to witness to Jesus, he or she is prepared. Because Christians can pray everywhere, they should try to be holy everywhere, refraining from talk and behavior that is crude, profane or disrespectful. To be holy is to take a stand against the evils in society.

We ponder the words of Benedict XVI: "And only where God is seen does life truly begin. Only when we meet the living God in Christ do we know what life is. We are not some casual and meaningless product of evolution. Each of us is the result of a thought of God. Each of us is willed, each of us is loved, each of us is necessary. There is nothing more beautiful than to be surprised by the gospel, by the encounter with Christ. There is nothing more beautiful than to know him and to speak to others of our friendship with him." In holiness, we remain perpetually in awe of Jesus Christ.

To be attentive to holiness, is to bond to that which lasts forever. Time and death cannot take it away. God is the creator of all that is good. The eternal realm is closer to the temporal realm than we can imagine. However, it is important to keep one's head out of the clouds. The Jesuit William Dych wrote, "The more one keeps both feet solidly on the ground, the better one can find God. To try to keep one foot in heaven and one foot on earth is to run the risk of being painfully pulled apart." Grace is a necessity for travel along the holiness trail, for getting to heaven and for helping others to get to heaven. When our feet are firmly planted on the ground, we can more easily see how everything is interwoven and connected to God. We are interdependent on each other.

Once upon a time, a little girl was lost in a large wheat field. The wheat was taller than she was. Her parents called in the neighbors to help find her, but all was in vain. Although they shouted and searched, they could not find the little girl. Finally, on the third day, the father said to the townspeople, "Let us all join hands and go through the field in a line." In no time, the child was found. Behind the plan was a common purpose. The child had to be found. The father gathered all the people who were willing to help. No one said, "I must tend to my crops," or "I have too many things to do." The neighbors immediately stopped whatever they were doing in order to pursue a greater good. They dropped their own ideas about how to find the little girl. They joined together and through a unified effort, found the lost child. God's mercy and love were made real by the neighbors.

No Two Alike

The saints are all around, in statues and pictures, in names of islands, cities, health care and educational institutions, and streets. The saints are very necessary as intercessors, as friends, as inspirations, as unique springs of wisdom and as the best models to follow. If God's bright white light was refracted into an innumerable array of colors, each saint would be represented by a few of those colors. Each color stands for something of God's attributes. Jesus invaded the life of each saint and to Jesus the saint said, "Welcome!"

Who among the saints would be a good friend for me? Pier Giorgio and John Paul II were rugged mountain climbers. However, the spiritual quest does not necessarily require immense strength, high energy or great vigor. Holiness is not confined to a station in life or specific personality traits. Goodness springs from all ambitions if a person continually asks for God's guidance and trusts in his providence. There were many saints who had poor health, among them Gemma Galgani, Bernadette Soubirous, and Faustina Kowalska. Paul of the Cross said, "Truly sickness is a great God given grace. It makes us discover who we are." Bearing illness or bad situations patiently can well be factors that make a person a saint. One can begin to find God in circumstances that are anything but favorable. People have connected with the divine in a prison or hospital as well as in a library or an open field. There is a wide and wonderful variety of saints, over ten thousand of them canonized, from Adelaide, a queen, to Zita, a servant. And there will be more to come.

No two saints are alike. Similar to flowers in the field, they are all different in color, size, shape and aroma. A dearly beloved saint, Therese of Lisieux, reflects: "In the world of souls, the living garden of the Lord, it pleases him to create great saints, who may be compared with the lilies or the rose; but he has also created little ones, who must be content to be daisies or violets." Augustine's life shows how it doesn't matter what one's past has been. He was a heretic who lived with a woman for fifteen years and fathered her son. He had a conversion experience and went on to become a most influential philosopher, theologian and doctor of the Church. Catherine of Genoa's husband was unfaithful and ill-tempered. He squandered their money to bankruptcy. Catherine endured and cared for the poor. Her husband saw the error of his ways, had a conversion and helped Catherine with her work with the destitute. Her writings, especially about purgatory, are insightful and comforting. Thomas More was a husband, father, lawyer, statesman and held a high governmental office. He had immense moral and religious courage. When he said no to the king he was beheaded. Benedict Joseph Labre was God's hobo. He was a misfit, vagabond, and in the world's terms a strange character and a failure. He had no one but God. He gave what little he had to others and spent much time in prayer before the Blessed Sacrament. He died homeless, on the streets of Rome at age thirty-five, most likely of malnutrition. When he died the people of Rome chanted, "E Morto il Santo," the saint is dead.

In her "Act of Oblation to Merciful Love," Therese of Lisieux wrote, "I desire, in a word, to be a saint, but I feel my helplessness and I beg you O my God to be yourself my sanctity!" She encourages us to be unafraid: "If you wish to be a saint, it is not hard. Have one aim, to please Jesus. . . . Love him who is love itself."

God calls a person to sainthood through his own unique design. John Ayscough said: "Every saint is a little looking glass of God; a facet of the jewel which constitutes the Catholic Church." Striving to be a saint is not all peaches and cream.

> If we were saints, we wouldn't have it easier, nor would we have special privileges, nor receive special gifts. The saints did not have it as easy as we would like to believe. They were men and women just as we are. They didn't live in greenhouses, isolated from temptation and sin. Otherwise their sanctity would have no special merit. They lived in the world as we do, and still served God in an extraordinary way. They loved the world: the aroma of a flower, the charm of an attractive animal, the confidence of little children, the friendship of mature men and women, and still won eternal life. They knew guilt and experienced the false way which the human heart travels. Still they asked for forgiveness. They fell, and committed the same mistakes. Yet they rose again and again

and thanked God who gave them the strength to do so. They also had bodies. They experienced within themselves the humbling weakness and inadequacy of human nature. Still they never forgot that they were children of God. The world was the workshop of their lives, but they never lost sight of the goal of their earthly pilgrimage—eternity.[2]

Shining for All

God's love shines in us and through us to others. The intensity of our light is a good measure of our love for Jesus and his Church. Holiness is dynamic, with a myriad of expressions that may change throughout one's lifetime. Great deeds do not necessarily mean advancement on the holy trail. This is usually made in small steps toward the holy, sometimes so small they can't even be seen. Stronger fidelity to God occurs when holiness shakes up the self satisfaction we can often develop toward our behavior and actions. Negative self discoveries can lead to positive change. Holiness is a clarion call that moves an individual from comfort and complacency to a yearning that cannot be fully satisfied and a search that is unceasing. Cursory religious practices deepen into communion with a God who is mystery. Images of God become ever changing, ever growing, until they finally disappear into God who is beyond all imaginative boundaries. Holiness is far from dull and boring! Rather, it keeps an individual ever watchful for the next good step, thus moving ever closer to God.

Holiness pushes us ahead, even though we may not have a clue regarding where we are going. Thomas Merton prayed:

> My Lord God, I have no idea where I am going. I do not see the road ahead of me. I cannot know for certain where it will end. Nor do I really know myself, and the fact that I think I am following your will does not mean that I am actually doing so. But I believe that the desire to please you does in fact please you. And I hope I have that desire in all that I am doing. I hope I will never do anything apart from that desire. And I know that if I do you will lead me by the right road, though I may know nothing about it. Therefore I will trust you always though I may seem to be lost and in the shadow of death. I will not fear, for you are ever with me, and you will never leave me to face my perils alone.[3]

---

2. Kelly, *Women before God*, 169.
3. Quoted from, *I Have Seen What I Was Looking For*. Thomas Merton (1915–1968)

This prayer illustrates how the pursuit of holiness is a journey from a known, limited landscape to an unknown, endless terrain. Moving forward begins to broaden a previously limited notion of who we think God is and what he expects of us. His eternal realm suddenly shines before and around us. We are guided by John Paul II: "Life, long or short, is a journey toward paradise. There is our fatherland. There is our real home. There is our appointment. Jesus is waiting for us in paradise. Never forget this supreme and consoling truth."

Truths of God transform lives. His burning light melts facades, masks, and pretenses and illuminates the true self. Sinfulness and powerlessness cause a person to be more dependent on God. Vices, anxieties, uncertainties and sins are faced without self-pity or discouragement, confident that "in all things God works for the good of those who love him, who have been called according to his purpose" (Rom 8:28). Although holiness has no simple definition, there is a reassuring constant. Every time we fall into sin, we must get up. Fall a thousand times, get up a thousand times is no small statement. Yes, holy people sin, but by the grace of God they get up, dust themselves off and try to do better. Sin has a strong tie with an enlarged ego. An increased ability to transcend self is a release from self-absorption. As we loosen our grasp on fulfilling our potential or actualizing ourselves, it frees us to discover the ingredients for spiritual growth in all of life's circumstances. By integrating the elements of spiritual development, a person develops an unpretentious transparency, an unobtrusive demeanor and an indisputable trust in Divine Providence.

Abiding in Jesus

In order to grow in holiness an individual must be firmly rooted in Jesus, the fruit of all holiness. "Abide in me and me in you. As the branch cannot bear fruit by itself unless it abides in the vine, neither can you unless you abide in me" (John 15:4). The more we see his light within us, the more we understand how central he is. He is the source that gives meaning and value to the many and diverse experiences in our lives, the rock on which we build our principles and practices, the inspiration from which we make our decisions and the singular star that guides our lives.

---

was an American convert. At the Abbey of Gethsemani in Kentucky, he was a Trappist monk, priest, hermit, poet, and prolific writer. His autobiography, *The Seven Storey Mountain*, was translated into over fifteen languages.

Come, be my guiding light, dear Lord,
A lamp unto my feet.
That I may ever follow you,
No other pathway seek.

To serve you with my heart and mind
In all I say and do.
And try to lead someone who's lost
To find their way to you.

May I give words that will uplift
Where hearts are sad today.
And may I not be slow to help
the needy on life's way.

To be thy faithful servant, Lord,
each day that dawns anew.
For heaven is the goal I seek
When earthly days are through.

And when my life draws to a close,
The hour, the day unknown.
Come, be my guiding light, dear Lord
And take me to thy home.

~Kay Hoffman

Quiet Places

Excessive busyness obstructs the ability to see who we are really meant to be. We barely know ourselves. Modern life often races past what is beautiful and life enhancing. When finding ourselves in this mode, it is imperative to slow down, pause, be still, be silent and listen. How is God helping us, leading us, blessing us? With help from God and others, we can work through all the unnecessary chaos. Esther de Waal wrote: "Unless I am silent, I shall not hear God, and until I hear God I shall not come to know God. Silence asks me to watch and wait and listen, to be like Mary in readiness to receive the Word. If I have any respect for God, I shall try to find a time, however short, for silence. Without it I have not much hope of establishing that relationship with God of hearing and responding which is going to help me root the whole of my life in prayer." Only in silence is the potential for holiness realized.

"Be still and know that I am God," the psalmist says. Silence and stillness whets the appetite for seeing the splendor of God's work in ourselves and, more importantly, in our souls. The soul has been called the fairest work of God. It is a haven for his loving, living flame, his Triune presence. The greatest sadness is souls so encrusted with sin that they are dead to the indwelling of the Triune God or to the exquisiteness of the soul. Silence and stillness are opportunities to become reacquainted with our soul. How beautiful she can be if we tend to her with great love. Silence and stillness are unfolding treasures that help to pass beyond rushing around in the outer realities of self-absorbed pursuits to roaming around in the inner reality of the soul. In this inner reality holiness reminders may take form in one's mind. When a siren is heard a Hail Mary is said for the people involved. A cross near the phone is a reminder to speak kindly to the caller, even bothersome telemarketers. A rosary held in the hand may well alleviate frustration and worry. Gazing at a holy picture or a religious statue may defuse an altercation or help with a tedious task. Repeating the names of Jesus, Mary and Joseph or saying the chaplet of mercy can lessen stress during a diagnostic test or while waiting in a doctor's office. Saying "All for Jesus" while doing unpleasant duties is a worthy custom. It was a custom for students in Catholic grade schools to write *JMJ*, for Jesus, Mary, and Joseph, at the top of their papers. People have received personal letters with *DV* written at the end of a sentence. DV means *Deo Volente* or God willing. *DOM* can also be an inscription, *Deo Optimo Maximo*, or to God, the best and greatest. The motto of the Jesuits can be noticed in many places: *AMDG, Ad majorem Dei Gloriam*, for the greater glory of God, or to strive to give God more glory by doing what is most pleasing to him. John Paul II frequently used the phrase "Praised be Jesus Christ!" These helps toward holiness are also reminders of divine assistance when temporal concerns seem to block the existence of heaven.

Holiness is simply a closer walk with Jesus. To walk with him is to discover our best selves. We live our best selves when we turn from negative thoughts, feelings and actions and face what is true, beautiful, good and life-giving. Finding our best selves in God develops a better communication with others. How we talk to others often reflects how we talk to God.

Communication with God is not a series of lofty thoughts, exalted insights, profound answers or deep consolations. It is much more than that. It is a deep surrender to our Creator, which allows God to tenderly embrace us. God opens hearts as spring opens beautiful flowers. In stillness and silence the flowers open, and so it is. At last, our heart has a small understanding about the splendor of our soul. Padre Pio gives us nourishment for our souls: "Prayer is the best weapon we have; it is a key that opens God's heart. You must speak to Jesus, not only with your lips, but also with your heart; actually, on certain occasions, you should speak with only your heart."

> Be born in us Incarnate Love!
> Take our flesh and blood and give us your humanity,
> take our eyes and give us your vision,
> take our minds and give us your pure thought,
> take our feet and set them in your path,
> take our hands and fold them in your prayer,
> take our hearts and give us your will to love.
>
> ~Caryll Houselander

To Reflect and to Witness

Bernard of Clairvaux said over a thousand years ago that action and contemplation are very close companions. They live together in the same house on equal terms. William Barclay, the scripture scholar, commented that the more one reads of the lives and works of dedicated men and women, the more one sees that they possessed two great qualities . . . the ability to work selflessly and the patience to wait in silence. In action and contemplation there is a blend in our lives: a rhythm of doing and resting, speaking and listening, giving and receiving. Prayer and quiet can increase our desire to spread the message and goodness of Jesus through our actions.

If we give appropriate time to "be" in our contemplative dimension, we have a better chance of being more attentive to "do" in the service of others. This is a marriage between the inner joy of listening to God and the outer joy of being his witness in the marketplace. Contemplation and action create a healthy tension. As we breathe in so must we breathe out.

A well-balanced Christian life naturally evolves into greater intimacy with God. How does this happen? Gradually the distance from him decreases because we become liberated from ourselves. Me is replaced by God. Catherine of Genoa once said, "My me is God, nor do I know my selfhood save in him." She had it right. "What can I do for God" becomes less important than "how can I 'be' in God." To "be" is to rest in God and quietly look at Jesus. A kinship in belonging to God takes place. It is refreshing. By loosening our grip on our own concerns, we become more accepting of the actions of God. We move from cognition about God to availability to God. Availability lets our doing take care of itself. There will always be things to do for God. We do what we can and disappear. We do not rest on our laurels, or wait for some goodness in return, but move on. A deeper settling into the realization that God loves us in a personal and infinite way is a sound sign of intimacy with God.

The touchstone of our journey into holiness is an unquestioning "yes" to Jesus' gentle inquiry, "Do you love me?" Our yes to God's love determines our ability to give and receive love. This affects people who touch the surface of our lives and those who are deep in our hearts. There is no journey in holiness without love. Saying yes to God provides strength to go beyond ourselves. We seek to see everything in God's love. When we view the world with eyes of love, it becomes rich and beautiful because we see it as opportunities for love.

The Apostle Paul said of Christ: "In Christ dwells all treasures and wisdom." John of the Cross offers a thought-provoking addition: "There is much to fathom in Christ for he is like an abundant mine with many recesses of treasures, so that however deep individuals go, they never reach the bottom, but rather in every recess find new veins with new richness everywhere."

Blessed are those who travel on the road of holiness, for it leads to Jesus. Indeed, it is a high road, but it is also the best road. So come, let us be on our way!

> Christ, be near at either hand,
> Christ, behind, before me stand.
>
> Christ, with me where e'er I go,
> Christ around, above, below.
>
> Christ, be in my heart and mind.
> Christ within my soul enshrined.

Holiness: Our True Identity

Christ control my wayward heart,
Christ, abide and ne'er depart.

Christ, my life and only way,
Christ my lantern, night and day.

Christ be my unchanging friend,
Guide and shepherd to the end.

~Irish folk song

Faith: The Eternity Connection

WHAT OPENS THE EYES of the heart and the ears of the soul? It is faith. Faith opens all eyes to see the wondrous love of God. Benedict XVI wrote: "Faith is foremost a personal, intimate encounter with Jesus. . . . It is in this way that we learn to know him better, to love him, and to follow him more and more." Church bells, sacred hymns, or a priest's homily are among the many ways to hear the call to faith. Deep faith is a profound respect and love for the truths of Jesus and his Church. This occurs when faith moves beyond superficial devotions, a cultural label, or rote reception of the sacraments. Faith is the most beautiful gift from God, and the most demanding.

If we are not rooted in faith, the strong winds of modern thinking will scatter us asunder. At times, it seems we are so buffeted by confusion, conflict and contradiction that we do not know what is happening. Many aspects of society hide the importance of God from humanity. There is so much activity, so many attractive new age programs, changing morals, popular movements and useless talk, noise and stimulation. What a challenge contemporary culture offers those of us who appreciate the sacred.

People have lost the ability to sit down and be quiet. The beauty of faith gently calls individuals away from the rapid pace and negative pull of society. An overactive contemporary life is a warning to sit down and ponder the prayer attributed to Cardinal Richard Cushing of Boston (1895–1968). Stillness begets an appreciation for the wonders of faith.

> Slow me down, Lord.
> Ease the pounding of my heart
> By the quieting of my mind.
> Steady my hurried pace
> With a vision of the eternal reach of time.

Faith: The Eternity Connection

Give me, amid the confusion of the day,
The calmness of the everlasting hills.
Break the tensions of my nerves and muscles
With the soothing music of the singing streams
That live in my memory.

Help me to know the magical, restoring power of sleep.
Teach me the art of taking minute vacations—
Of slowing down to look at a flower,
To chat with a friend, to pat a dog,
To read a few lines from a good book. . . .

Remind me that there is more to life
Than increasing its speed.
Let me look upward into the branches
Of the towering oak and know that it grew great and strong
Because it grew slowly and well.

Slow me down, Lord,
And inspire me to send my roots deep
Into the soil of life's enduring values
That I may grow toward the stars
Of my greater destiny.

    Faith is a gift, always a gift. Many people do not open this gift. Their greatest poverty is not knowing God. With the help of grace from the Holy Spirit, we respond to this gift with every choice we make each day of our lives. How do our choices reflect our belief in God? How does our lifestyle resonate with the attributes of Jesus? We must live what we profess.

    To state views assertively, with forethought and grace, and to support human rights without infringing on the rights of others are sure signs of being steadfast in faith. Saying things others want to hear or being a people pleaser does not fit into the teachings of Jesus. When an individual lives the teachings of Jesus well, she receives so much more than she gives.

    Another steadfast sign of faith is to be a promise keeper. Marianne, a young wife and mother, planned to make a retreat. She promised three friends she would give them a ride to this retreat. These women were filled with joyful anticipation. However, a few days before the retreat, Marianne received an invitation to meet Mother Teresa, and it was on the same weekend as the retreat. Marianne had really wanted to meet a "living saint" ever since she was a young girl. She felt conflicted. However, she knew she had made a commitment and that a promise is a dreadful thing to break. She prayed and declined the invitation.

In the quiet of the retreat chapel Marianne realized that there were saints all around her. Her retreat companions looked normal; there was nothing outstanding about them. However, there was an unexplained peace and joy radiating from these women. Was this intangible something sanctity? We are reminded by Anthony of Padua: "The saints are like the stars. In his providence, Christ conceals them in a hidden place that they may not shine before others when they might wish to do so. Yet, they are always ready to exchange the quiet of contemplation for the works of mercy as soon as they perceive in their hearts the invitation of Christ."

Faith is lived with an upright heart and hard work. In other words, to believe in Jesus is to do what he commands. Faith is ever watchful. We watch what we say: Is it necessary? Is it true? Is it kind? Augustine, a bishop and Doctor of the Church, advises us: "Do not rejoice in earthly reality, rejoice in Christ, rejoice in his word, rejoice in his law. . . . There will be peace and tranquility in the Christian heart, but only as long as our faith is watchful; if, however, our faith sleeps, we are in danger."

Pilgrim's Progress

God's faithful pilgrims make the love and goodness of God visible on earth. The holiness in their lifestyle counteracts and diminishes the power of sin and evil. Belief in God is a serious, sacred trust that grows stronger as long as there is growth in holiness. Faith is the prime motivator that gives witness to God in words, action and conduct. The best response to God and his love is an increase in faith. Faith is actualized by prayer, participating in the liturgy, receiving the sacraments, living a virtuous life and serving others. Faith filled decisions and actions stir up the desire to continually seek the Triune God and abide by his word. We live our faith through the teachings of our religion, a sound and sturdy guide. Living the tenants of religion goes hand in hand with respecting others for their religion beliefs.

> I grew up in a very Protestant area. The majority of the populace belonged to a Lutheran sect that was at best wary and at worse downright bigoted when it came to Catholics. There was no

parochial school attached to our little mission church so we few Catholic kids merged with our Lutheran neighbors on buses, bikes or on foot each day to make our way to the public school. Most days you couldn't tell a Catholic from a Lutheran, but when Lent came along the distinctions became noticeable. The Catholics were recognizable by the black smudge of ashes on their foreheads. The Catholic kids generally didn't eat candy during the week but instead hoarded it away for consumption on Sunday which didn't count as a day of Lent. The Catholics could not eat meat on Friday during Lent and here's where egg salad sandwiches take on significance.

Two mothers were assigned to provide a lunch for our classroom parties throughout the year. These parties were always on a Friday afternoon when our eagerness to be free for the weekend pretty much obliterated any possibility of learning. Since kids are always hungry, the lunches were pretty substantial—not just a snack. It seems there was always a party or two during Lent and typically the room mothers would have been of the Lutheran faith. Even though their church did not require abstinence from meat on Fridays, they never forgot that the little Catholic kids would need special consideration and they went to the extra effort of providing egg salad for us so that we would not be left out when the plate of sandwiches was passed. It was a kindness that I have never forgotten.[1]

Head and Heart

John of the Cross advises: "Faith lies beyond all understanding, taste, feeling, and imagining that one has. However impressive may be one's knowledge or feeling of God, that knowledge or feeling will have no resemblance to God and amounts to very little. To attain union with God, a person should neither advance by understanding, nor by support of one's own experience, but by belief in God's being." Faith declares what the senses do not perceive. We believe what we do not see and in the end we will be rewarded by what we have believed. "Blessed are those who have not seen and yet believe" (John 20:29). David Spangle tells us: "Faith, to me, is the capacity to be open to the intangible, invisible domains of life. It is the ability to be comfortable in the presence of mystery. It is the willingness to go where

---

1. Pat Nyquist, OSB, in *Spirit & Life* magazine (Benedictine Sisters of Perpetual Adoration, Tucson, AZ), March/April 2007.

the senses cannot always take us, to appreciate and be open to the realm of energy and spirit. Faith creates an open space in which the unexpected, the unpredicted, and often the most essential can appear and become known."

When Christians pass through the door of faith, they enter the highest realm of their existence: the spiritual life with the Triune God as described in the *Catechism of the Catholic Church*. God is our Father who created us. Jesus is his son who shows us the way to the Father. The Holy Spirit helps us along this way. And at the end of this earthly sojourn we enter into eternal life. Faith forms a heart into a sanctuary because it is the dwelling place of the Holy Trinity. We can visit this sanctuary and see the fire of faith still burning. These little visits can keep our lamp of faith alight when we are working, studying, eating or resting.

It is more important to believe than to understand. Too much conversation can dilute the mysteries of faith. Excessive explanation can reduce the richness in the symbols of faith. If someone stops to explain the why behind the lighting of the candles at Mass, when this is taking place, it stops the graceful flow of this ritual. To reverently complete the ritual and trust that the ritual will give its own teaching, will not disturb the beauty of the moment. An explanation can be given after Mass. Talking about something cannot take the place of living it. Faith is more authentic when it is the key to life, rather than the subject for dialogue.

Thomas Merton tells us, "Ultimately, faith is the only key to the universe. The final meaning of human existence, and the answers to the questions on which all our happiness depends cannot be found in any other way." When faith matures, questions about Christian beliefs are replaced with a wonderment in the mystery of God and the beauty of his truth. A sense of awe replaces a relentless search for that which is unknown or not understood. New manifestations of the mystery of God are not seen as a source of pride but as a deepening in humility. The truths of faith are beyond human cognition and will only be fully understood in heaven. The limits of knowledge are not roadblocks to knowing God better. Intellectual ability can become a source of pride. Rationalization justifies thoughts and conduct through human reasoning alone. Therefore, it can lead to justifying erroneous thinking, producing good reasons to do bad things, or good reasons for not doing good things we are supposed to do. Mature faith is not based on great intelligence or noteworthy scholarship. It is based on assiduous prayer and belief in the truths and mystery of the Triune God.

Faith: The Eternity Connection

Over a hundred years ago, a university student was walking through a quiet park. He saw an elderly man sitting on a bench alone and sat down next to him. The elderly man was praying the rosary, moving the beads with his fingers. "Sir, do you still believe in such outdated things?" asked the student of the old man. "Yes, I do. Do you not?" asked the man. The student burst out laughing and said, "I do not believe in such silly things. Take my advice. Throw the rosary away and learn what science has to say." "Science? I do not understand this science. Perhaps you can explain it to me." The student saw that the man was deeply moved. So to avoid hurting the feelings of this man he said: "Please give me your address and I will send you some literature." The man fumbled in the inside pocket of his coat and gave the student his visiting card. On glancing at the card, the student bowed his head and became silent. On the card he read: Louis Pasteur, Director of the Institute of Scientific Research, Paris.

Faith rises above the limits of that which is known and into the realms where intelligence cannot go. Loving God is greater than knowledge about God because God's love is greater than what we are able to know. It seems incomplete to describe Jesus within the boundaries of human thoughts, culture and language. Metaphors and allegories fall short. Letting loose of attempts to explain God assists in surrendering to his tremendous mystery. Angela of Foligno, a thirteenth-century Franciscan Italian mystic wrote: "I have known with certitude that the more one has a sense of God the less one can speak of God. The more one has the feeling of infinity and the ineffable the more one lacks words for it." Faith elevates a Christian to greater goodness and helps maintain a pristine soul. There is no love or hope without faith. Faith is the root of good works, which flowers in love through the fruit of action. Indeed, faith in the Catholic tradition is the keystone for a very good life.

> Faith of our fathers living still,
> In spite of dungeon, fire and sword;
> O how our hearts beat high with joy
> Whenever we hear that glorious word:
>
> Faith of our fathers, holy faith,
> We will be true to thee till death.
>
> Our fathers chained in prisons dark,
> Were still in heart and conscious free,

And blest would be their children's fate,
If they, like them, should die for thee:

Faith of our fathers holy faith,
We will be true to thee till death.

Faith of our fathers! We will love
Both friend and foe in all our strife;
And preach thee, too, as love knows how,
By kindly words and virtuous life:

Faith of our fathers, holy faith,
We will be true to thee till death.

~Frederick William Faber
(1814–1863)

Twilight Times

The gift of faith includes mystery, which is so necessary when seeking God in positive or negative life situations. To focus on the light of God's truth and the hope of heaven while walking through the shadows is an enormous blessing. Faith reassures us that God is with us even when we walk through a seemingly trackless wasteland. When out of sorts for one reason or another, there is peace in the fact that this shall pass. Faith is an energizer that strives to uniquely reflect the image and likeness of God in all of life's circumstances. When we ponder his love and mercy, how little we know! Thinking about his greatness and majesty keeps the concerns of life in their proper perspective.

"Faith is a gift from God allowing us to enter peacefully into the dark night which faces every one of us at one time or another. Faith is at peace, and full of light. Faith celebrates the very warp and woof of one's existence. Faith considers that its precariousness and its finiteness are but the womb in which it abides, moving toward the plenitude and fullness of the eternity which it desires and believes in and which revelation opens to it." So wrote Catherine de Hueck Doherty. Faith is a stronghold when suffering shakes up our lives. With faith, there is a certain peace in suffering because faith deepens love and unites our personal suffering with Jesus' suffering. Grace keeps us moving along the bumpy road of life. God is not responsible for adverse events along this road. His goodness is found through these events when they teach us humility, forgiveness and repentance. How sweet are the ways of faith. With our significant faults we repeatedly sin and fall. Nevertheless, we take Jesus' hand and get up quickly. We are forgiven and Jesus continues to inspire and guide us. We are not discouraged and continue to try to live as good Christians again and again and again.

Faith is the sanctuary of peace on a wayfarer's journey. In his book *He Leadeth Me*, Walter Ciszek, SJ, wrote:

> Only by a lively faith can a man learn to live in peace among the tensions of this world, secure in his ability (with God's help) to weather the crises of life, whenever they come and whatever they may be, for he knows that God is with him. In the midst of suffering or failure, or even sin, when he feels lost or overwhelmed by danger or temptation, his faith still reminds him of God. By faith he has learned to lift himself above the circumstances of this life and to keep his eyes fixed upon God, from whom he expects the grace and the help he needs, no matter how unworthy he may feel. Faith, then, is the fulcrum of our moral and spiritual balance. The problems of evil or of sin, of injustice, of sufferings, even of death, cannot upset the man of faith or shake his trust and confidence in God. His powerlessness to solve such problems will not be a cause of despair or despondency for him, no matter how strong his concern and anxiety may be for himself and for those around him. At the core of his being there exists an unshakable confidence that God will provide, in the mysterious ways of his own Divine Providence.[2]

In divine faith, the one believed is God. In human faith, the ones believed are persons. It is sometimes challenging to accept the word of another in honesty and in truth. Thomas Aquinas wrote: "Someone may object that it is foolish to believe what he cannot see. . . . Yet, life in this world would be altogether impossible if we were to believe only what we can see. How can we live without believing others? How is a man to believe that his father is so and so? Hence man finds it necessary to believe others in matters that he cannot know perfectly on his own."

Faith and its necessary sacrifices are an essential part of love within families, between friends and in the Church. As trust and faith in God is strengthened, it increases trust and faith in others (within reason). It

---

2. Ciszek, *He Leadeth Me*, 186.

provides a foundation for accepting others, which includes those we do not understand (our children) or like (our neighbor, supervisor or in law).

Holy Surprise

A life of faith can be ignited from a small grace such as a quiet reading of the Twenty-Third Psalm, a beautiful sunset or something someone said. On rare occasions, it can be ignited by an extraordinary occurrence and lead to unimaginable places. In the beginning of his book *The Waters of Siloe*, Thomas Merton relates this story:

> It is late at night. Most of the Paris cafes have closed their doors and pulled down their shutters and locked them to the sidewalk. Lights are reflected brightly in the wet, empty pavement. A taxi stops to let off a passenger and moves away again, its red tail light disappearing around the corner.
>
> The man who has just alighted follows a bellboy through the whirling door into the lobby of one of the big Paris hotels. His suitcase is bright with labels that spell out the names of hotels that existed in the big European cities before World War II. But the man is not a tourist. You can see that he is a businessman, and an important one. This is not the kind of hotel that is patronized by mere voyageurs de commerce. He is a Frenchman, and he walks through the lobby like a man who is used to stopping at the best hotels. He pauses for a moment, fumbling for some change, and the bellboy goes ahead of him to the elevator.
>
> The traveler is suddenly aware that someone is looking at him. He turns around. It is a woman, and to his astonishment she is dressed in the habit of a nun. If he knew anything about the habits worn by the different religious orders, he would recognize the white cloak and brown robe as belonging to the Discalced Carmelites. But what on earth would a man in his position know about Discalced Carmelites? He is far too important and too busy to worry his head about nuns and religious orders—or about churches for that matter, although he occasionally goes to Mass as a matter of form.
>
> The most surprising thing of all is that the nun is smiling, and she is smiling at him. She is a young sister, with a bright, intelligent French face, full of the candor of a child, full of good sense, and her smile is a smile of frank, undisguised friendship. The traveler instinctively brings his hand to his hat, then turns away and hastens to the desk, assuring himself that he does not know any nuns.

As he is signing the register he cannot help glancing back over his shoulder. The nun is gone. Putting down the pen, he asks the clerk, "Who was that nun that just passed by?" "I beg your pardon monsieur. What was that you said?" "That nun, who was she anyway? The one that just went by and smiled at me." The clerk arches his eyebrows. "You are mistaken, monsieur. A nun, in a hotel, at this time of night? Nuns don't go wandering around town, smiling at men!" "I know they don't. That is why I would like you to explain the fact that one came up and smiled at me just now, here in this lobby." The clerk shrugs: "Monsieur, you are the only person that has come in or gone out in the last half hour."

Not long after, the traveler who saw that nun in the Paris hotel was no longer an important French industrialist, and he did know something about religious habits. In fact, he was wearing one. It was brown: a brown robe, with a brown scapular over it, and a thick leather belt buckled about the waist. His head was shaved and he had grown a beard. And he wore a grimy apron to protect his robe from axle grease. He was lying on his back underneath a partly disemboweled tractor. There was a wrench in his hand and black smudges all around his eyes where he had been wiping the sweat with the back of his greasy hands. He was a lay brother in the most strictly enclosed, the poorest, the most laborious, and one of the most austere orders in the Church. He had become a Trappist in a southern French abbey.[3]

God No Matter What

In the grand scale, life is not as serious as people think it to be. Life is holy and valuable in its ordinariness as long as folks are forthright and define themselves by faith rather than by successes and accomplishments. The things that diminish Christian identity also diminish insights, creativity and energy. The way individuals relate to God has a distinct connection with the way they respect others. The dignity they display toward others and themselves reflects the respect they have for God.

We strive to live by faith no matter what happens in life. Faith is believing in that which is unseen, and is the foundation for a sound self-image so basic to life. It is the light that guides our days when our days are like nights and nothing makes sense. It sustains a sense of security amid all the ambiguities of life. Yet, faith can be difficult. In her book *Sister Wendy on*

3. Merton, *Waters of Siloe*, 13–14.

Prayer, Sister Wendy Beckett gives us this illustration to help us along: "The holiest person I know has never had the slightest interior intimation that God exists. All she gets back from her prayer is doubt and darkness. She experiences a terrible fear that her life with God is all imagination, that there is no God, that living as a nun is a mockery. With this agonizing sense of her own personal weakness and her own absolute absence of felt certainty, she chooses. She chooses to believe. She chooses to act in accordance with that belief, which means in practice a life of heroic charity. This woman—and others like her, because she is not alone in this heroism—is giving to God the real sacrifice of faith. This woman chooses to love God and to serve him and to believe in him, even if she gets noting back. It is a glory to know that she exists and that there are others like her."

Mary is the unsurpassed example of a faith-filled person. She shows that with God nothing is impossible. She welcomed the angel Gabriel's message. "Be it done unto me according to your word" is a response to say each day of our lives. All through the circumstances and events of her life, Mary continued to say "yes." Her faith never wavered. She shows all people how to know and love Jesus better. She helps everyone understand Jesus who cannot be contained or limited by human definitions. She shows people how to pray by opening their minds and hearts to the power of the Holy Spirit. In order to be students in her school of faith, it is mandatory to deeply understand the need for silence, recollection and how to live and grow in faith by being responsive to the mystery of God in ordinary life. Mary walks ahead of us as we walk through the dark confusion of our time. The light from her lantern of faith helps us see situations with trust in the Lord. She is forever reassuring that Divine Presence is always with us. Mary is the best of all role models there is to show everyone the myriad of beauties along the road of holiness and most of all, the magnificent beauty of her son.

> Mary, help of Christians,
> Hasten to our aide:
> Pray for us in sickness
> To your Son who died:
> He who healed the lepers
> Will not fail to heed
> You, his honored mother,
> Bearer of our need.

Faith: The Eternity Connection

Mary, help of Christians,
Hear our urgent pleas
For your wounded children,
Broken and diseased:
He who bled to heal us
Will not fail to heed
You, beloved mother
Bearer of our need.

~*Magnificat* magazine, February 2011

Hope: Evergreen

C. S. Lewis wrote:

> My own experience is something like this. I am progressing along the path of life in my ordinary, contentedly fallen, and godless condition, absorbed in a merry meeting with my friends for the morrow or a bit of work that tickles my vanity today, a holiday or a new book, when suddenly a stab of abdominal pain that threatens serious disease, or a headline in the newspaper that threatens us all with destruction, sends this whole pack of cards tumbling down. At first, I am overwhelmed, and all my little happinesses look like broken toys. Then, slowly and reluctantly, bit by bit, I try to bring myself into the frame of mind that I should be in at all times. I remind myself that all these toys were never intended to possess my heart, that my true good is in another world and my only real treasure is Christ. And perhaps, by God's grace, I succeed, and for a day or two become a creature consciously dependent on God and drawing its strength from the right sources. But the moment the threat is withdrawn, my whole nature leaps back to the toys. I am even anxious, God forgive me, to banish from my mind the only thing that supported me under the threat because it is now associated with the misery of those few days. Thus the terrible necessity of tribulation is only too clear. God has had me for but forty-eight hours and then only by dint of taking everything else away from me. Let him but sheathe that sword for a moment and I behave like a puppy when the hated bath is over—I shake myself as dry as I can and race off to reacquire my comfortable dirtiness, if not in the nearest manure heap, at least in the nearest flower bed. And that is why tribulations cannot cease until God either sees us remade or sees that our remaking is now hopeless.[1]

---

1. C. S. Lewis, *The Problem of Pain*, quoted in Groeschel, *Journey toward God*, 78–79.

Does this scenario remind us of someone? With today's continual development of new technological toys, people can become destructively self-absorbed. They neglect, or do not believe in, God. They live for the here and now, and their hope ends at the grave.

Hope is not wishful thinking or unfounded expectation. It embraces the plenitude of the present as well as the possibilities for the future. Hope is essential for taking appropriate risks that go beyond safety and security. Christian hope gives us confidence in the goodness and love of God, and in his ultimate triumph. Jesus suffered and we suffer; he died and we shall die; he struggled with good and evil in his forty days in the desert, and we struggle. So, despite the calamities the future holds, hope gives us the interior peace and strength to shoulder whatever comes our way. Christian hope is a blessed gift.

One day a young sister was walking with an older, seasoned sister in the convent garden. Feeling insecure about what God wanted her to do; she was asking the older sister for some advice. The older sister walked up to a rosebush, handed the young sister a rosebud and told her to open it without tearing off any petals. The young sister looked in disbelief at the older sister as she was trying to figure out what a rosebud could possibly have to do with wanting to know the will of God regarding her ministry. Because of her great respect for the older sister, she proceeded to try to unfold the rose, while keeping every petal intact. She quickly realized how impossible this was to do. Noticing the younger sister's inability to unfold the rosebud without tearing it, the older sister began to recite the following poem:

> It is only a tiny rosebud, a flower of God's design. But I cannot unfold the petals with these clumsy hands of mine. The secret of unfolding flowers is not known to such as I. God opens this flower so easily, but in my hands they die. If I cannot unfold a rosebud, this flower of God's design. Then how can I have the wisdom to unfold this life of mine? So I'll trust in God for leading each moment of my day. I will look to God for guidance in each step of the way. The path that lies before me only my Lord knows. I'll trust God to unfold the moments, just as he unfolds the rose.

Hope helps us leave the flowers of our life in the hands of God. When Christians believe God is in control, hope springs eternal. There is an assurance that this is God's world and he is more concerned about the people in it than they are. Hope is not a naive optimism, but rather a disposition that accepts challenges and suffering as a part of life. Although aware of character weaknesses and having no illusions about sin, a Christian is full of hope. The Christian way recognizes sin and does not despair because the Holy Spirit continues his work with each individual and leads him or her by the hand, very gently, toward the Father's house.

Candlelight

A lighted candle often represents hope. When prayer seems as cold as ice or as dark as night, an individual can gaze at a candle flame. Candles come in different shapes and sizes. The large Paschal candle stands alight at Mass during the Easter season, at baptisms and at funerals. It represents the victorious Christ who leads his followers through their days and nights. There are Advent traditions of lighting a candle in the window to guide Mary and Joseph into one's home, and lighting candles on the Advent wreath. Christmas candles celebrate Jesus' birth and light the way for the wise men to come and see him. Lighted votive candles represent prayers. A simple candle flame is a brilliant symbol of hope. It keeps the chill of darkness at bay by giving us light and warmth. Like birds that sing in the dark before the dawn, flames are a reminder that the sun will rise. May these flames of hope always show the way to the flame in the Christian heart, which is a perpetual reminder of Christ the light.

> It is in that holy moment
> when the candlewick is snuffed
> and the yellow halo grows
> its black cord
> that the warm wax works its
> softness into us,
> wraps its way around our hearts, like the climbing smoke
> from the extinguished candlewick
> up the staircase of air—
> that moment of unmistakable nasality
> of candle scent in chapel dark
> that suffers us to realize
> that we are to be trimmed to burn again.[2]

---

2. *Spirit & Life* magazine (Benedictine Sisters of Perpetual Adoration, Tucson, AZ) May/June 2012.

Christ Our Light

Christians live in the light because of the reassurance that Christ is risen and is directing the world to its final destiny. With Jesus' help, fears are recognized, but they no longer dominate the days since there is strength in believing in Jesus and his promises. Death is the testament to, and final expression of, hope. Without hope in God, humankind will not reach its fullest potential. Teresa of Avila[3] reminds us: "Hope, O my soul, hope. You know neither the day nor the hour. Watch carefully, for everything passes quickly, even though your impatience makes doubtful what is certain, and turns a very short time into a long one. Dream that the more you struggle, the more you prove the love that you bear your God, and the more you will rejoice one day with your Beloved, in a happiness and rapture that can never end." It should not be "I think, therefore I am" but rather, "I believe, therefore I always will be." Herman Melville writes: "Hope is the struggle of the soul, breaking loose from what is perishable and attesting to her eternity." Christians believe in the greatness and blessedness of eternity even though it is shrouded in mystery and only partially revealed. Yes, eternity has extraordinary descriptions, but while on earth, they can only be understood as fragments of a whole. Hope, rooted in faith, is the means by which a person trusts in God, and that God will grant eternal life as long as an individual abides by the tenants necessary to attain that life. It is essential to do what is required and to rely on God's infinite goodness and promises in order to reach humanity's ultimate destiny.

A Golden Thread

Hope is a thread that should be woven through a life, not simply stitched into occasional patches with a few cheery words or scattered good deeds. Hope sustains optimism, the belief that something better can be attained. In his *Summa*, Thomas Aquinas said that hope is an activity concerned with a future good that is difficult to accomplish, but that is capable of achieving, with the help of God. Hope puts all in the hands of God with confidence. To

---

3. Teresa of Avila and her associate, John of the Cross, were Spanish Carmelites in the sixteenth century. They brought to the Church a new expression of the ancient rule of Our Lady of Mount Carmel. Followers of that expression became known as the Discalced Carmelite nuns and friars. Teresa and John are time honored and highly respected masters of the spiritual life, practical mystics and Doctors of the Church. Their books are spiritual classics that continue to have a universal appeal today.

maintain hope when a situation appears to be hopeless takes strong faith. "But they that hope in the Lord shall renew their strength, they shall take wings as eagles, they shall run and not be weary, they shall walk and not faint" (Isa 40:31).

A hope-filled soul lifts thoughts and aspirations to something beyond the physical or mental self. With confidence in God, new ways are found toward the positive and the good. Everything a person does impacts humanity in a positive or negative way. Hope is reflected in one's thoughts, words and actions. Sweet are the graces that come from having an orientation of hope.

> Gladys Aylward, a missionary to China more than fifty years ago, was forced to flee when the Japanese invaded Yuncheng. With only one assistant, she led a hundred orphans over the mountains toward free China. During the journey she grappled with fear. After passing a sleepless night she faced the morning with no hope of reaching safety. A thirteen year old girl in the group reminded her of their much loved story of Moses and the Red Sea. "But I am not Moses," Gladys sighed in despair. "Of course you aren't," the girl said, "but God is still God!" When Gladys and the orphans made it through to freedom, they proved once again that no matter how inadequate we feel, God is still God, and we can still trust him. Sometimes God calms the storm, other times he lets the storm rage and he calms us. Either way, he sustains us and brings us through. We always have a choice: either we give the burden to God or we try to carry it ourselves. How does God provide for us? One day at a time. Remember the Israelites in the wilderness? Each day God fed them by sending manna from heaven. Notice how it worked. The number of people in each family determined the amount of manna they received, no more and no less. And God would only enable them to collect enough for each day; hoarded manna rotted. Trust God for today and leave tomorrow in his hands. "Give your burdens to the Lord, and he will take care of you."[4]

In His Heart

Faith can be called a gift of fire in the heart and hope has been called a sure and steadfast anchor of the soul. Neither faith nor hope can exist without the other. Together they keep Christians moving on the spiritual journey.

---

4. United Christian Broadcasters (UK), *Word for Today*.

Without faith and hope alive within Christians, they cannot encourage faith and hope in others. They are like wings that take humankind to the Heart of Jesus. Jesus urges Christians onward: "Ask and it will be given to you; seek and you will find; knock and it will be opened to you" (Luke 11:9).

An anchor, with a crosspiece at the top of the shaft, has been a sign of hope since the days of the early Christians. This sign was often carved on the tombs of the early Christians in the Catacombs of Rome. The anchor symbolized that the deceased buried there had reached the port of eternal salvation or heaven. Paul wrote in Hebrews 6:18–19: "Hold fast to the hope we set before us which we have as an anchor for the soul." Before the fifth century, a dolphin or two fishes were near the crossbar. The cross on the anchor symbolized Jesus, a code known to Christians, but not to unbelievers. In religious art, the anchor represented hope, courage, safety and confidence.

There is always a safe harbor in the Sacred Heart. This beloved image is very familiar to us; it is the well-loved symbol of Jesus' immense and all-consuming love for humankind. This unsurpassed love is our anchor and our refuge. The Heart of Christ exemplifies ultimate selfless love. The Sacred Heart gives us whatever help we need to take the next good step. Jesus said he will be with us. He is the best of companions in our little boat.

Kahlil Gibran wrote: "Say not God is in my heart, but rather say I am in the Heart of God." Jesus invites all humankind to take refuge in his Heart. To dwell in his Heart is to dwell in his goodness and his love. The Heart of Jesus looks upon people more mercifully than they can look upon themselves or others. If individuals place their hearts in the Sacred Heart of Jesus, they love together with the love of Jesus. This is an excellent way to learn to love better. Only in Jesus can Christians find a Heart capable of loving to the fullest extent of love. The strength of Jesus' Sacred Heart keeps the waters of grace flowing in the Church and in the world. Christians become part of that river of living water by meeting the needs of society through doing God's will. Christians strive toward seeing others as God sees them, and willing the good that God desires for them. This opposes the popular notion of love which pursues self indulgent pleasure.

The Best Way to Start the Day

To stay on the path of hope, an excellent practice would be to recite the Morning Offering as soon as one gets up in the morning. As a reminder to do this, it would be prudent to post this prayer on the bathroom mirror or closet door:

> O Jesus, through the Immaculate Heart of Mary, I offer you my prayers, works, joys, and sufferings of this day in union with the Holy Sacrifice of the Mass throughout the world. I offer them for all the intentions of your Sacred Heart: the salvation of souls, reparation for sin, and the reunion of all Christians. I offer them for the intentions of our bishops and of all Apostles of Prayer, and in particular for those recommended by our Holy Father this month. Amen.

Father Walter Ciszek, SJ, was imprisoned in the Soviet Union under Joseph Stalin's regime. Through his great suffering he found the Morning Offering an uplifting grace. "Father Ciszek experienced day after day that saying the Morning Offering helped him see the profound truth about God's will for his life. Offering his own sacrifices with the sacrifice of the Mass gave them meaning. He found out that hopelessness came from injecting too much of self into life. It was his experience that we worry too much about what we can or cannot do, but we can do God's will, and doing that restores hope."[5]

> In every life there's a pause
> That is better than onward rush,
> Better than hewing or mightiest doing;
> 'Tis the standing still at Sovereign will.
>
> There's a hush that is better
> Than ardent speech,
> Better than sighing or wilderness crying;
> 'Tis the being still at Sovereign will.
>
> The pause and the hush sing a double song
> In unison low and for all time long.
> O human soul, God's working plan
> Goes on, nor needs the aid of man!
> Stand still, and see! Be still, and know!
>
> ~V. Raymond Edman
> "Blessed Calm"

---

5. Smith, *Homilies*, xxv.

Within the still, silent milieu of Jesus' Heart one can sit in his presence and drink in his wisdom. When we offer ourselves to God the Father in the Heart of Jesus we become, along with our weaknesses, faults and limitations, a sign of the holiness of God and of hope to others. In the Heart of Jesus, a Christian is inspired and uplifted by his great love. Uniting our human hearts with the Sacred Heart will help make all of us channels of hope and visible signs of God's merciful love to humanity.

The Mystical Body

Each Christian is part of Christ's mystical body the Church. As the Apostle Paul wrote, the body of Christ is made up of many parts. Each person is a cell within this body. The blood of Christ, which pulses from his Sacred Heart, nourishes and energizes all Christians so that they strive to live in hope and contribute to the good of humanity. Jesus' Heart beats for humanity's salvation and is pierced by humanity's sins. Choices by humanity range from contributing to the well-being of the mystical body to fighting against it. To choose the latter is to become like diseased cells in the body of Christ. If the latter is chosen a Christian can seek reunion by praying and receiving spiritual direction and the sacraments, thus becoming a healthy cell once again.

It is regrettable to remain permanently angry with the Church because of some dispute with a priest, a parish, or a doctrine. If all the facts were known it could be possible that there was no reason for the dispute in the first place. Negative ruminations can drain energy, destroy hope and increase bitterness. What are the real reasons behind a dispute? Could it be ignorance, misinformation, laziness, or a strong attachment to one's own opinion? It takes courage to uncover authentic truth. When deeply hurt by a priest, religious or lay member of the Church, it takes a high degree of inner strength to say, and to truly believe, the words of Jesus: "Father forgive them for they know not what they do."

Jesus is the King, and the Church is a kingdom of sinners, Jesus is the Shepherd, and we are the straying sheep, God is the Father, and Christians are his wayward children. The Church isn't a country club for the elite, it is a hospital for sinners. The Church is a family. Members can be frustrating, scandalous, irritating; they will never be perfect. But, when things go wrong, family members do not give up on each other. As Peter said: "To whom shall we go?" Jesus is one with his Church. When he appeared to Saul he didn't say, "Why are you persecuting my Church?" He said, "Why are you persecuting me?" The Church is the mystical body of Christ. Benedict XVI said: "Despite human weakness, despite difficulties and trials, the Church is guided by the Holy Spirit, and the Lord will never fail to give his aid in sustaining the Church on her journey." The Catholic Church is a fascinating, ancient, complex, living, global, mystical, jocular, solemn, enchanting bride of Christ.

Mater et Magistra

The central purpose of the Church is to praise the Triune God, and to assist in making people holy. G. K. Chesterton compared the Church to a house with a thousand doors. And inside these doors we see a diversity of saints, scholars, scientists, educational and health care institutes, artists and their religious masterpieces, musicians and their inspirational music, holy places, holy families, religious orders, secular institutes and much, much more. At the center of this house stands Jesus with his loving Heart and open arms, saying, "Come to me." Ever exploring this wondrous house, the Christian realizes the harmful effects of brooding about past situations, and instead pays attention to present discoveries, for above each door are the words "Hope to all who enter here."

The Church is much more than an institution, a system of legalistic rules, or hierarchy. It continues the mission of Jesus and fosters a way of life that sustains sound morals, purpose, and direction toward that which is most noble, most beautiful and most sacred to the human person. A Catholic life lived rightly can be an intimate walk with God. As Paul wrote to the Philippians, "Whatever is honorable, whatever is just, whatever is pure, whatever is lovely, whatever is gracious, if there is any excellence and if there is anything worthy of praise, think about these things" (Phil 4:8).

John Henry Newman wrote:

> Trust the Church of God implicitly even when your natural judgment would take a different course from hers and would induce you to question her prudence or correctness. Recollect what a hard task she has; how she is sure to be criticized and spoken against, whatever she does; recollect how much she needs your loyal and tender devotion; recollect, too, how long is the experience gained in 1800 years; and what right she has to claim your assent to the principles which have had so extended and triumphant a trial. Thank her that

she has kept the faith safe for so many generations and do your part in helping her to transmit it to generations after you.[6]

A Christian walks into an old, quiet Catholic church and may see the flicker of candle flames in a rack, each flame representing a prayer. Someone may be saying a rosary at Mary's altar, someone else making the Stations of the Cross, yet another praying quietly at the back of the church. All is hushed in an atmosphere of otherworldliness. Years ago the Church was referred to as Holy Mother Church, and rightly so. She is the haven from the hurts on earth. She is like a mother who holds her young child's hand as they cross a busy street. These days we need a strong mother who protects and defends us from the exigencies of modern society. Be careful, she says to us. Remember we are children of God and somehow things work out if we do our best and trust in Divine Providence. Christians should not be overwhelmed with the mechanics of the Church. Rather they must see the Church as the channel for the message, mission and mystery of Jesus. It isn't the what of externals around us, but the who of Jesus within us. Holy Mother Church is wise and holy, she wants her children to get to heaven and she has been around for a long, long, long time. Indeed, the Church is our mater et magistra, our mother and teacher.

> In April of 2005 the newly elected pope Benedict XVI came onto the front loggia of St. Peter's Basilica to bless the crowds. Gathered around him on the adjoining balconies there appeared all of the cardinals who had just chosen him. The news cameras caught the remarkably pensive expression on the face of Cardinal Francis George of Chicago. When the cardinal returned home, reporters asked him what he was thinking about at that moment. Here is what he said: "I was gazing over toward the Circus Maximus, toward the Palatine Hills where the Roman Emperors once resided and reigned and looked down upon the persecution of Christians,

---

6. Quoted from Newman's *Idea of a University*. John Henry Newman was born in London, and became the 19th century's most important English-speaking Roman Catholic theologian. He spent the first half of his life as an Anglican and the second half as a Roman Catholic. In both churches he was a priest, popular preacher, writer, and eminent theologian. He published eight volumes of *Parochial and Plain Sermons*, two novels, and poems. In 1845, he was received into the Catholic Church. Two years later he was ordained a Catholic priest in Rome and joined the Congregation of the Oratory, founded three centuries earlier by St. Philip Neri. Newman wrote forty books including his autobiography, and 21,000 letters that survive. Newman was named a cardinal in 1879, his motto was "Cor ad cor loquitur" (Heart speaks to heart). His name is linked to ministry centers at many public and private colleges and universities in the United States.

and I thought, Where are their successors? Where is the successor of Caesar Augustus? Where is the successor of Marcus Aurelius? And finally, who cares? But if you want to see the successor of Peter, he is right next to me, smiling and waving at the crowds."[7]

Dark before the Dawn

Christians will experience barren trees on their holiness landscape. There will be times when all seems cold and dark. If there is a feeling that time spent in spiritual pursuits is squandered, Sister Wendy Beckett responds: "Body and soul may feel we are wasting our time. Hope smiles and ignores them." The light in hope is an inspiration to find God's grace in the dark problems of life. Without hope, hearts would easily break. Adversities of many kinds are a part of life. People spend much time praying that their troubles will end. However if they do not, God can change the way people look at them. Hard times can bring people closer to Jesus, increase love and hope and be a channel to a bare-bones trust in God. Sometimes it seems as if our little flame of hope has been blown out. However, we must remember that it is possible to find God when life becomes thoroughly confusing or disappointing, when all is mystery, and when we are in the depths of pain. We are human, and at times, it is common to think about "what if. . . ." What if I lose my health, fail this test or lose my job? This type of thinking takes us to the bottom of the valley of the shadow. "What if" negatives can shut a person down.

> The earth lies cold and dark,
> and blackened trees
> are sentinels of silhouetted
> loneliness against the bleak, stark nakedness of day.
> Unwarmed, unwelcome,
> I make my way through
> landscape damp and chill:
> even the birds are silent;
> even the trees are still!
> I listen to my heavy step:
> I hear no other thing,

---

7. Barron, *Catholicism*, 35.

Hope: Evergreen

> 'Til out of grey curtained distance,
> a bluebird and chickadee sing!
>
> ~Carmel of Terre Haute

Joan was asked by a sister friend to visit a woman named Isabelle who was in a psychiatric hospital. She was without family or friends. Hospital policy permitted only family visits, but the charge nurse let Joan visit one time for ten minutes. Isabelle's eyes showed great sadness and desolation. As Joan prepared to leave she quietly told Isabelle that she was special and much loved by God. Afterward, Joan wrote regular encouraging notes to Isabelle. They were short uplifting words about how Jesus loves her or biblical verses of support. Joan also prayed for Isabelle. A year later, there was a knock at Joan's front door. She opened the door but did not recognize the woman. It was the patient she had visited in the psychiatric hospital. This time her eyes showed peace and happiness. Isabelle thanked Joan for her visit and notes. She saved all of them, and let Joan know how her support helped her get out of the hospital. Isabelle read the notes over and over because they gave her hope when she had no hope.

Hope opens up human hearts. Like curtains slowly parting to admit a winter dawn into a home, hope allows beams of light to make their way into the hearts of humankind. Even when standing in cold darkness, hope reveals a verdant landscape beyond our present desolation. Hope lifts thoughts out of the dark valley toward the inner flame of light. We look forward and move forward to that which gives us a reason to live. Hope brings beauty to a repugnant environment and sustains sanity during intolerable times. Viktor Frankl, in his classic book *Man's Search for Meaning*, which was based on his experience in Nazi concentration camps, shows how most people who hold on to the hope of achieving something positive can survive the worst of human conditions. To believe that something good will be fulfilled is a strong incentive for life. Indeed, living in hope is healthier than living in fear. To share darkness with God will help change things for the better. The less people rely on their own strength, the more they depend on grace from the Holy Spirit. Moments alone with him in the dark storms of life are significant benchmarks in our growth. Dark nights will pass. Even though a person may think he is alone, he knows God does not leave him. God is within, mysteriously, ambiguously, elusively, and beyond comprehension. God cannot be harnessed, but a person can increasingly surrender to him. We trust him in the darkness. Mysteries from the dark surprise us: We become content in a simple lifestyle, love God more for himself than for the gifts he gives and learn more about our faith. Indeed, hope keeps the wolves of discouragement, loneliness or abandonment from howling at the door.

"Dark and cold we may be, but this is no winter now. The frozen misery of centuries breaks, cracks, begins to move. The thunder is the thunder of the floes, the thaw, the flood, the upstart spring. Thank God our time is now when wrong comes up to face us everywhere, never to leave us till we take the longest stride of soul men ever took. Affairs are now soul size, the enterprise is exploration into God" (Christopher Fry).

New Spring

"It is only with the heart that one can see rightly. What is essential is invisible to the eye" (Antoine de Saint Exupery).

> Something spring like remains with me in these weeks following heart surgery, something that suggests the kind of person I wish to be for the rest of my life. An incident in these first weeks has become a symbol of the tiny shoot pushing from old soil. When I left intensive care, my nurse gave me a little pillow made by hospital volunteers. She apologized, however, because mine, unlike "adult" pillows, was covered with figures of a little bear looking at a flower. He wore a yellow shirt, short red pants, and a smart blue hat with a yellow visor. At the time, I felt only the softness of the pillow against my chest. A few days later, the little fellow became my companion.
>
> I was much like a child in the hospital. I did not try to impress anyone with my bravery. Being defenseless, exposed, and dependent, I held the little pillow close to my chest or face, not caring what anyone thought. I experienced, however fleeting, the susceptible attitude and posture that is all too quickly forgotten in the defensive adult world. With my little pillow, I remained a child, mostly helpless, full of wondering and tears, which I welcomed as lost companions. I expected I would graduate from the pillow, but I notice even now that I know exactly where it is at any time. If I wish to take a nap, it is all I need to put me to sleep. Last year when I saw many in Oklahoma City hugging teddy bears at the barricades or in the televised memorial service, I knew in my head what they were doing. Now I understand with my heart.

The other day in cardiac rehabilitation I was pumping away on an exercise bike when an older man entered the room to inquire about the program. He was accompanied by his wife and another woman, perhaps his daughter. Dressed in dark clothes, he wore an indifferent look on his face, blank, hidden. My first reaction was to turn away. Then I noticed that he was clutching one of the little pillows. The way he clung to the pillow betrayed the indifference and detachment on his face. Immediately I felt my pain and his and how much we both were in need of consolation and reassurance. I wanted to get off my bike, go over to him, and tell him that his pain and fear were going to work out ultimately. I looked at him, loved him, but for the same reasons that he came into the room wearing an emotionless look, I kept on pedaling. Many times since then I have thought about both of us and what keeps us and the world apart. I think about my distance from others, and I remember the little pillows we all clutch.

If only we could see the hidden pillows being carried by those we pass on the street, persons whose controlled faces give no hint of vulnerability, yet who filled with fear, clutch at the pain inside them and wonder about their lonely lives. If only we would overcome decorum, self protective habit and security, and get off our machines to hold them.

Spring's child is exposed, susceptible, precarious willing to admit pain, fear, and hope. She is unashamed to clutch her tiny pillow openly and be who she is. For now though, I use my pillow primarily to soften my ribs as I turn in sleep. I do not think that I have learned all I can from it. It is, after all, a pillow for my heart, not my plugged arteries. It is a reminder to take life into my heart and arms, and press it close, even as a child holds a stuffed animal in the face of threat and fear.[8]

Our Life, Our Sweetness, and Our Hope

As she lived her life as a wife and mother, Mary is our exemplar of the highest hope and complete trust in God. She walked in faith and in mystery, but maintained a deep peace. She came and went quietly, her house was undistinguished among the others in her village. She tended the fire, scoured the earthenware vessels, trimmed the lamps, cooked and sewed. The secret of her hope was that her daily mundane tasks were accomplished with great love and confidence in God's plan for her. In the evenings, we can

---

8. Marv Hiles, *The Daybook: A Contemplative Journal* (Spring 1996).

imagine her holding Jesus close to her heart, still pondering, and perhaps softly singing a lullaby as Joseph quietly whittles a wooden toy for him.

Hope was Mary's stronghold. She held onto it in times of great concern, and there were many. After giving birth to Jesus, she traveled in haste to Egypt. While on another journey, she lost her son. Like most women of her time, she worked from dawn to dusk. She was a widow at an early age with a teenage son. She watched helplessly as Jesus was cursed and spit upon, and stayed with him during his agony and death. Mary lived with a vision of hope rooted in faith. Hope drew her beyond herself, her fears and her worries. God was the tower of strength to whom she clung no matter what happened. She kept moving forward even though she did not understand what was happening. She lived the will of God perfectly, and urges us to do the same. The will of God is our sanctification. Therese of Lisieux, who gave us the little way to Jesus, makes this more accessible: "I hope in him who is virtue and sanctity itself. He alone, content with my frail efforts, will lift me up to himself, clothe me with his own merits and make me a saint."

We are here to spread love and hope as Mary did. Mary was concerned about others. The bride and groom at Cana ran out of wine and quietly, without drawing attention to herself, Mary did something about it. To see with the eyes of Mary is to see the needs of others in our home, church and community, and to address them in quiet, loving ways. As Mary is the woman of hope, so we must try to be signs of hope to others. A kind deed, positive word or gentle smile can spark hope in the heart. Mary is our strength as we help others navigate through these confusing times. It is a sacred duty to replace anguish with hope, anxiety with peace, indifference with love, ugliness with beauty and an earthly vision with a heavenly one. Gregory of Nyssa wrote: "Hope always draws the soul from the beauty that is seen to what is beyond, always kindles the desire for the hidden through what is perceived."

"We ask you Mother of Christ, to be our guide to the Heart of your son. We pray to you, lead us close to him and teach us to live in intimacy with this Heart, which is the fountain of life and holiness."[9]

---

9. John Paul II, Angelus Address, September 6, 1986.

Love: That Which Makes the World Go Round

THERE IS AN EBEN Holden Christmas story about a little boy who got two shillings from his father for Christmas. He walked to Salem to spend it. While trying to decide what to buy, he saw a tiny girl in a red jacket looking at dolls. She appeared very poor and sickly. She would go up to a doll, put her hand on it and say, "Some day! Some day!" She asked the clerk if she had a doll for three pennies. "No," said the clerk, "the least for any doll with a dress is a shilling." It looked as if the little girl was going to cry. "Some day I'm going to have one," she said. The boy couldn't stand it any more, so he bought a doll and put it in her arms. The boy never forgot the look that came over her face. Well, she went away and sat down all by herself. Later that night they found her asleep in an alley, half dead with cold, but she had taken off her little red jacket and wrapped it around the doll. "Did she die and go to heaven?" asked a child who was listening to the story. "No, she lived and went to heaven. You've crossed the boundary when you begin to love somebody more than you do yourself, even if it isn't anybody better than a rag doll."

Taking care of someone, or something, be it a person, pet, garden or a rag doll takes us out of ourselves. Sacrifice is love's highest expression. Love, a sweet fruit in season at all times, has many manifestations. How do I define love? Today the word "love" is frayed at the edges from overuse. It is associated with so many trivial things. Ernest Holmes presents a broad view on the subject. "Love is the lodestone of life, the great and supreme reality, the highest gift of heaven, the greatest good on earth, the treasure of all our search. While hate kills, love renews and invigorates. As love is the greatest healing power, no one feels whole without it. Love need not be confined to only a few, but can be extended to many without losing the love of a few. In fact, when love becomes more complete it will take in a larger and larger territory and in doing so experience a greater degree of livingness."

What a wonderful reflection on love. It is worth pondering. Yet something is missing, the source of love: God. We cannot keep going without God. No one can love us like he loves us. His love sustains us, not because we earned it, but because his love is all merciful.

We belong to God. If we really think about this phrase, it is both awesome and comforting. God is the source of the most exquisite form of love known to humankind. To belong to God is to be incorporated into his love which is so much greater than our love. In his treatise on spiritual perfection, Diadochus of Photice wrote:

> Anyone who loves God in the depths of his heart has already been loved by God. In fact, the measure of a man's love for God depends upon how deeply aware he is of God's love for him. When this awareness is keen it makes whoever possesses it long to be enlightened by the divine light, and this longing is so intense that it seems to penetrate his very bones. He loses all consciousness of himself and is entirely transformed by the love of God. Such a man lives in this life and at the same times does not live in it, for although he still inhabits his body he is constantly leaving it in spirit because of the love that draws him toward God. Once the love of God has released him from self love, the flame of divine love never ceases to burn in his heart and he remains united to God by an irresistible longing.[1]

If we truly belong to God, we try to adhere to his love in the daily aspects of our lives. The energy that comes from belonging changes us. The love of God means to love what is good. Clare of Assisi explains aspects of love: "We become what we love and who we love shapes what we become. If we love things, we become a thing. If we love nothing, we become nothing. Imitation is not a literal mimicking of Christ, rather it means becoming the image of the beloved, an image disclosed through transformation. This means we are to become vessels of God's compassionate love for others." Loving people and things for their own good keeps personal energy, intentions and yearnings within a wide, life-sustaining love for the greater good of humanity. This is far from the narrow use of people and things for selfish gratification. God is not too concerned about the make of my car, the size of my house, the brand names of my clothes, my job title, salary or the number of friends I have on Facebook. He is more concerned about the

---

1. *Liturgy of the Hours*, 3:101.

number of people I gave rides to who did not drive. How I made people feel welcome in my home. How I clothed the poor. What percentage of my salary I gave to the needy or how I helped my distraught friends.

Pure and Simple

Therese of Lisieux wrote: "Just as the sun shines at the same time on cedar trees and on each little flower as if it was the only one on earth, so does our Lord takes special care of each soul as if it was his only care." Little flowers and little children can teach us about love. The famous children's TV personality Mr. Rogers once gave a talk that included something that had happened at the Seattle Special Olympics. There were nine contestants, all of them physically or mentally challenged, for the 100 yard dash. All of them were assembled at the starting line. At the sound of the gun they took off. Not long afterward one little boy stumbled, fell, hurt his knee and began to cry. The other eight children heard him crying, slowed down, turned around and ran back to him. One little girl with Down syndrome bent down, kissed the boy and said, "This'll make it better." The little boy got up. He and the rest of the runners linked their arms together and joyfully walked to the finish line. They all finished the race at the same time. And when they did, everyone in the stadium stood up, clapped, whistled and cheered for a long, long time. Such spontaneous expressions of love are beautiful to observe and receive. God must smile when he sees such sweet expressions of love. We are all lovable because God loves us. We love God, and love others because of God. When his love animates us, the legitimate concerns of others become our concerns. Love cannot be confined to words; it must be expressed in good will. Gregory the Great challenges us:

> There is nothing we can offer to God more precious than our good will. But what is good will? To have good will is to experience concern for someone else's adversities as if they were your own; to give thanks for our neighbor's prosperity as for our own, to believe that another person's loss is our own, and also that another's gain is ours; to love a friend in God, and to bear with an enemy out of love; to do to no one what we do not want to suffer ourselves, and to refuse to no one what we rightly want for ourselves; to choose to help a neighbor who is in need, not only to the whole extent of our ability, but even beyond our means. What offering is richer, what

offering is more substantial, than this one? What we are offering to
God on the altar of our hearts is the sacrifice of ourselves.[2]

Love is serving a cause greater than personal needs. Wouldn't it be wonderful if all humanity would link arms and help each other to the finish line?

Ever Moving

Love has so many ingenious ways of stretching people beyond the vision they have for themselves. Simple signs of love are the best. Therese of Lisieux reminds us, "Little things done out of love are those that charm the heart of Christ . . . the most brilliant deeds, when done without love are but nothingness." We serve meals to the homeless with a smile and we serve meals to those with whom we live with a smile. We strive to maintain a home where God is loved and honored even when the family lacks a similar spiritual enthusiasm. We are the example for family members to love, help and care for each other to the best of their ability. Love begins at home, with us. Sometimes routine tasks like cleaning, washing or taking out the garbage are annoying. What if we hum a tune, think a happy thought or remember lines of a poem while doing these tasks? Therese said, "Love can accomplish all things. Things that are most impossible become easy where love is at work. . . . When in the morning we feel no courage or strength for the practice of virtue, it is really grace. It is time to rely on Jesus alone." A random act of love can take us out of ourselves and into the heart of Christ.

> Love divine, all love excelling,
> Joy of heaven, to earth come down!
> Fix in us thy humble dwelling,
> All thy faithful mercies crown.
> Jesus, thou art all compassion,
> Pure unbounded love thou art;
> Visit us with thy salvation,
> Enter every trembling heart.

---

2. Pope Gregory I, *Be Friends of God*, 65. Gregory the Great was elected pope of the Catholic Church in 590 and he is also a Doctor of the Church. He is famous for initiating the first recorded large-scale mission from Rome, the Gregorian Mission, to convert pagan people to Christianity. Gregory is also well known for his writings, which were more prolific than any previous pope. Gregorian chant was named after him.

> Breathe, O breathe thy loving spirit
> Into every troubled breast;
> Let us all in thee inherit,
> Let us find thy promised rest.
> Take away the love of sinning;
> Alpha and Omega be;
> End of faith, as its beginning,
> Set our hearts at liberty.
>
> ~Charles Wesley
> (1707–1788)

When it is nourished by prayer, and rooted in Jesus, love is the inspiration that gives life value and directs hearts toward the good of humanity. It is the power that keeps a person praying for the betterment of society or keeps a person at the bedside of a sick loved one. God's love helps an individual move forward in trust when the future seems uncertain. It empowers us with the ability to accept life's unexpected changes with peace, to move forward through successes, mistakes, and discouragement without anxiety. John of the Cross advises: "Like the bee that sucks honey from all the wildflowers and will not use them for anything else, the soul easily extracts the sweetness of love from all the things that happen to her, that is, she loves God in them. Thus everything leads her to love always the delight of loving God."

Rose

It is not uncommon for the expression of love to change as the years pass. A dramatic example is the life of Rose Hawthorne Lathrop. She was born in Lenox, Massachusetts, in 1851, but spent her childhood years in Liverpool, England, because her father, Nathaniel Hawthorne, was the US counsel there. She came home to Concord, Massachusetts, in 1860. Rose married George Parsons Lathrop when she was twenty; they settled in Boston. George worked at the *Atlantic Monthly* and Rose established her reputation as a writer by publishing short stories and poems. After five years, a son, Francis Hawthorne Lathrop, was born, but he died of diphtheria when he was only five years old. Rose and George were both received into the Catholic Church in 1891, ten years after their son's death. When George developed problems with "intemperance" he could no longer hold a job and their marriage become intolerable. With her confessor's authorization, Rose began to live by herself, took nurse's training and started work with patients suffering from incurable cancer. This was a heartbreaking ministry to which she devoted the rest of her life. After George's death in 1898, Rose became a Dominican sister and with other like-minded women established the Dominican Congregation of St. Rose of Lima, also known as the Servants of Relief for Incurable Cancer. Their first center for cancer patients was established in Hawthorne, New York, where Mother Mary Alphonsa, OP, Rose's religious name, spent the rest of her years. She died there in 1936. Rose was a lady of culture, education and social status who put on an apron and used the gifts from her abundance to serve Christ's poor. She lived among the poor, begged for them, and established several homes where they could live their final days in dignity, ease, cleanliness and peace. There was no class system between the residents and religious sisters. The sisters were true servants and the residents were recipients of their care and concern.

Rose and others like her show us that love must have adaptability. They exemplify Thomas à Kempis's words:

> Love often knows no measure, but burns white hot beyond all measure. Love feels no burden and counts up no toil; it aspires to do more than its strength allows, it does not plead impossibility, but considers it may do and can do all things. So it finds strength for anything; it completes and carries through great tasks where one who does not love would fail and fall. Love is vigilant, it sleeps without losing control; it is wearied without exhaustion, cramped without being crushed, alarmed without being destroyed. Like a living flame or a burning torch, it leaps up and safely passes through all. When a man loves, he knows the meaning of that cry that sounds in the ears of God from the burning love of the soul: My God, it cries, my love! You are wholly mine, and I am wholly yours![3]

Who is our neighbor? Our neighbor is the one who needs us the most. Teresa of Avila said, "Though we do not have our Lord with us in bodily presence, we have our neighbor, who, for the ends of love and loving service, is as good as our Lord himself." What is truly valuable is not what

---

3. *Imitation of Christ*, bk. 3, ch. 5. Thomas à Kempis, also known as Thomas Hamerken (1380–1471), was a German-Duch priest, monk, and canon regular of the late medieval period. *The Imitation of Christ* has been translated into over fifty languages and is one of the most well-known Christian devotional classics, still popular today.

we have but who we love. Rose's life illustrates how love seeks the good of others. She stepped outside of her safety zone to serve the suffering. At times it is difficult to overcome that which keeps us from loving service. Love strives to be deaf to unkind remarks and blind to small faults. Love helps us see others as brothers and sisters even when they spit or scream at us. Therese of Lisieux guides us: "Perfect love means putting up with other people's shortcomings, feeling no surprise at their weaknesses, finding encouragement even in the slightest evidence of good qualities in them." She also said: "When we have to deal with a disagreeable character, let us not lose heart and let us never give up."

Lux in Tenebris

An old Native American story is told about a grandfather who said to his grandson: "I feel like I have two wolves fighting in my heart. One wolf is mean spirited, angry and attacks everything. The other wolf is forgiving, loving and kind." "Which wolf will win the fight in your heart?" the grandson asked. "The one I feed," said the grandfather. Which wolf do we feed?

Love is like lux in tenebris, light in darkness. Just as the flicker of a sanctuary lamp in a dark church symbolizes the presence of Christ in the tabernacle, so do acts of love symbolize the love of Christ in a sin-dark society. The greatest challenge is to bring the light of holiness to the dark areas in society. An openness to God encourages choices toward loving service to others. As visible signs of God's love, we should behave in a way that reflects the light of Christ in all we say and do. This, in turn, brings out the best in others. Our behavior often influences others without our knowing it because we do not know who is watching us. The way one manages life communicates one's level of holiness. A positive orientation is a great asset. One simple word of encouragement can inspire someone to do something good, give hope, or help someone overcome fear and uncertainties. Love is at its best in small, unknown expressions. Teresa of Calcutta[4] encourages us: "It is not the magnitude of our actions, but the amount of love that is put into them that matters." Love is the reason behind kind gestures and patience toward others. John of the Cross said, "He that with pure love works for God not only cares not whether or not

---

4. Mother Teresa (1910–1997) founded the Roman Catholic religious congregation Missionaries of Charity. She and her sisters have devoted their lives to serving the poor and destitute around the world.

men know it, but he does not even do these things so that God himself may know it. Such a person, even though it should never be known, would not cease to perform these same services and with the same gladness and love." Think about visiting an aged relative or friend in a nursing home. We are committed to this, sometimes without the feelings to motivate us. If we relied on feelings, we would easily make excuses to avoid those visits. There are times when we do not feel like going, or have the heart for such a visit, but we go anyway. From time to time we may experience some sense of satisfaction, but we should not depend on that. The most important aspect is that we are steadfast in our visits.

It is such a blessing when simplicity and respect take the place of confusion and neglect. It is more beneficial to admire and be grateful for the things of God than to be harsh and critical of the human condition. We choose to build up or tear down. Holiness is a manifestation of personal authenticity and God centered existence while striving to excel as followers of Jesus. Colossians 3:12-14 reads: "As God's chosen ones, holy and beloved, clothe yourselves with compassion, kindness, humility, meekness and patience. Bear with one another.... Forgive each other.... Above all, clothe yourselves with love, which binds everything together in perfect harmony."

A story is told about an old man and a young man who took part in a special program. During part of this program, each man was to repeat from memory the words of the Twenty-Third Psalm before a large audience. The young man was trained in the best speech and drama techniques, and, in the language of an ancient silver-tongued orator, said the words of the psalm. When he had finished, the audience gave him a standing ovation and asked him for an encore, so they could hear again his wonderful voice. Then the old gentleman, leaning heavily on his cane, walked to the podium. In a feeble and shaking voice, he repeated the same words. When he sat down, no sound came from the audience. They seemed to be in prayer. In the silence, the young man returned to the podium and quietly said, "Friends, I wish to make an explanation. You asked me to come back and repeat the psalm, but you remained silent after my friend was seated. The difference? I shall tell you. I know the psalm, but he knows the shepherd." Such are the ways of love.

To dwell upon the Triune God abiding within awakens a tender, longing love for him. The older man knew the tenderness of God's love in a personal way. In time and with grace we realize that God is the only one who can really satisfy our deepest longings. We must be still with God,

Love: That Which Makes the World Go Round

settle down in his company, let him love us and trust in his Providence. Although we recognize love, we never completely understand it.

> Love bade me welcome; yet my soul drew back,
> Guilty of dust and sin.
> But quick-ey'd Love, observing me grow slack
> From my first entrance in,
> Drew nearer to me, sweetly questioning
> If I lacked anything.
>
> "A guest," I answer'd, "worthy to be here";
> Love said, "You shall be he."
> "I, the unkind, ungrateful? Ah, my dear,
> I cannot look on thee."
> Love took my hand, and smiling did reply,
> "Who made the eyes but I?"
>
> "Truth, Lord; but I have marr'd them; let my shame
> Go where it doth deserve."
> "And know you not," says Love, "who bore the blame"
> "My dear, then I will serve."
> "You must sit down," says Love, "and taste my meat."
> So I did sit and eat.
>
> ~George Herbert

Merciful Love

Before we can give love to others, we must be open to love working within ourselves. We are made for reverent love. It is the greatest gift to ever give or receive. Beautiful graces come from love. It is liberation from many damaging negative traits. Love gives the strength and courage to do things never thought possible. We are ever grateful for God's love for us, which impels us to love others. Love is a calling to understand people who hurt us and to trust they will become what God intends them to be. This is a great and continual challenge that we take on with hope.

The grace received from God's loving mercy is in proportion to our mercy toward others. Therefore, when the mercy of God is received, it must be passed on. A most important component of mercy is forgiveness. It is surprising how often we are called to forgive. This happens within a family, between friends, in church and on the job. Small daily works of mercy should be routine. Easy forgiveness keeps the work running smoothly. Forgiving, forgiving and more forgiving, without measure and without count, creates the foundation on which mercy is built.

The thin space that should be between God and us thickens like a dense fog when we sit on our pity bog and ruminate about our grievances. Authentic love includes forgiving those who trespass against us. Forgiveness is manifest when the evil that has been done is no longer a barrier between us and the person who hurt us. Have we forgiven the irritating people in our lives: the annoying neighbor, the obnoxious in-law, the abusive parent who has been dead for eight years? Grudges drag us into the dark pit and perpetuate negative thoughts, so what is the use of holding on to them? How often do destructive thoughts about the wrongs done to us circulate in our mind? Are we a captive of our grudges and bitterness or our desire for revenge? This only wears us down. We must look past our retributions and leave vengeance to God.

Forgiveness is good soul care. If we forgive others, and ourselves each day, it is easier to love and be loved. When we examine the health of our soul, what do we find? A visible proof of love for God and the common good is to keep his commandments. Thomas More wrote: "If our love for something causes us to break God's commandment, then we love it better than we love God, and that is a love both deadly and damnable." Sin freezes people within the confines of their egos. Augustine said sin is a state of being caved in on oneself. Sins remain sins no matter how society, or cultural mores, define them. A word, deed or desire that opposes God's law, and therefore his love, is a sin. Sins cannot be justified as minor faults, softened by semantics, or justified by clever rationalizations. A sin remains a sin no matter what people call it or how often other people do it. Striving for holiness requires being honest about our sins and fully confessing them. Through the act of contrition we tell God we are deeply sorry for our sins and ask him to give us strength to resist tempting situations. We do the penance the priest gives us and add acts of reparation to make up for our sins and the sins of others. To partake often of the Sacrament of Reconciliation is a great blessing. Confession is good for the soul.

Perseverance in prayer and straightforward forgiveness should be routine parts of our day. We must work on forgiving easily because we ourselves are in desperate need of forgiveness. There is no limit to the number of times God can forgive us. There should be no limit to the number of times we forgive ourselves and those who hurt us. It comes down to this: If we do not forgive, we are not forgiven. Forgiveness needs to be a daily habit because in addition to healing broken relationships, it sanctifies, reconciles, and strengthens the body of Christ.

Merciful love can be as attractive as it is difficult. It cultivates forgiveness, kindness, goodness and service in our relationships. It also is a clarion call to hard tasks, like sowing good seed in an enemy's field. Johann von Schiller wrote, "As freely as the firmament embraces the world, so mercy must encircle friend and foe." President Lincoln was asked how he was going to treat the rebellious Southerners after they were defeated and returned to the Union of the United States. The president said, "I would treat them as if they had never been away." This is mercy. To let go of the evils that have been done to us is not easy. However, Jesus calls us to forgive, always. This way of life keeps us looking up in hope and moving forward in grace. Jesus' mercy is always available to us. Our ability to forgive does great good for our hearts by connecting us with the sublimity of God and serving as conduits of mercy to others.

In his book *High Wind at Noon*, Allan Knight Chalmers tells us about the extraordinary story of Peer Holm, who was a world-famous engineer. He built great bridges, railroads and tunnels in many parts of the world; he gained wealth and fame, but later came to failure, poverty, and sickness. He returned to the little village where he was born and, together with his wife and little girl, eked out a meager living.

> Peer Holm had a neighbor who owned a fierce dog. Peer warned him that the dog was dangerous, but the old man contemptuously replied, "Hold your tongue, you cursed pauper." One day Peer Holm came home to find the dog at the throat of his little girl. He tore the dog away, but the dog's teeth had gone too deeply and the little girl was dead.
>
> The sheriff shot the dog, and the neighbors were bitter against his owner. When sowing time came they refused to sell him any grain. His fields were plowed but bare. He could neither beg, borrow, nor buy seed. Whenever he walked down the road, the people of the village sneered at him. But not Peer Holm. He could not sleep at night for thinking of his neighbor.
>
> Very early one morning he rose, went to his shed, and got his last half bushel of barley. He climbed the fence and sowed his

neighbor's field. The fields themselves told the story. When the seeds came up, it was revealed what Peer had done, because part of his own field remained bare while the field of his neighbor was green.

Mercy requires that we sow good seed in our enemy's field, even though it means that part of our own field will be left bare. It is not easy. It is the hardest possible action, but it is our key to God's kingdom.[5]

> Teach me to love, Lord, as you love,
> Make it unconditional, honest and kind,
> To ask nothing back in return, Lord,
> To encompass the whole of mankind.
>
> May I offer my love without speaking,
> May it radiate as it shines forth from me,
> May it be seen in my face and my eyes Lord,
> May it be simple, sincere, and shame free.
>
> Show me how to forgive, Lord, as you do,
> To not burden another with guilt,
> To not play the role of the martyr,
> To be a rock on which trust may be built.
>
> Make my love for others be greater by far
> Than any love that is offered to me,
> Led by thy Spirit, inspired of God,
> As forgiving as Jesus. . .and free.
>
> ~Virginia Ellis[6]

---

5. Allen, *God's Psychiatry*, 146–47.

6. From the *Christopher News Notes*, 503, an inspirational pamphlet regularly published by the Christophers, a Christian organization founded in 1945 by Father James Keller, headquartered in New York. The name is derived from the Greek word meaning "Christ bearer." Their motto is: "It is better to light one candle than to curse the darkness."

Discipleship: Following Jesus

Before the term "Christian" was used, Christians were known as followers of "the way." The way was, and is, Jesus Christ. After Jesus restored sight to the blind man, that man followed Jesus on "the way." Jesus himself said, "I am the way." This way has a direction and goal: to live, move, and have our being in Christ. There will be many paths that depart from the way and lead people astray. However, even though they glitter and shine with sweet expectations, disciples try not to wander off from the way, because it is the way of ultimate truth. A Christian pilgrim's life begins in God and will end with God through the guidance and wisdom of Jesus.

What does it mean to follow Jesus in the twenty-first century? How does being a Christian apply to daily existence? Each day, decisions are made to stay on his way. Richard of Chichester wrote: "Day by day, day by day, O dear Lord, three things I pray: To see thee more clearly, love thee more dearly, follow thee more nearly day by day." Saints are saints because they followed Jesus day by day. Their examples have become guideposts on our way to God. By God's grace, saints evolved into all God created them to be. Each saint is a unique image of Christ in the world. To follow Jesus is to be serious about becoming our own brand of a saint. Jesus is the unsurpassed leader in this adventure in holiness.

Jesus became man for all. He invites all people to follow him and helps them to become fully human. The greatness of humanity is found in Jesus. There is no greater challenge on this earth than to follow Jesus. He is the foundation for how to live, how to forgive and how to love. Christian spirituality does not lessen a person's humanity; it takes humanity to its highest level. To be a Christian is to grow more like Jesus. To be a Christian is to take the person, teachings and life of Jesus seriously. Christians are not removed from the world and its problems. They bring Christ into the world by infusing his teaching into society. Remaining close to Jesus is living faith through a manner of life based on the discipline of religion. To instill the beauty of the incarnate God into working and living places is a noble task. People come to know Jesus by Christians who are living the gospel. The Holy Spirit is teacher and guide in this sacred trust. The Holy Spirit keeps Jesus' presence alive in the heart, especially when daily duties and responsibilities occupy the mind.

Disciple means one who is learning, a pupil or follower. To be a disciple of Jesus is to respond to the call to follow him. Jesus calls people in many different ways. The secret of growing in discipleship is to listen attentively and respond faithfully to what we believe Jesus is asking. We are always learning how to respond to his calls. A commitment to Jesus is a commitment to growing in knowledge about Christ, responding to grace, and being indelibly changed by him. To live his message is to be a channel for healing, peace and love for all. We abide with Jesus, adhere to him and work with him doing good in his name. Standing up for Christ means encouraging hope in others, extending compassion without condescension and serving without need for appreciation. Love is the glorious gift of the Risen Lord to share with others by respecting their dignity. Although this is so necessary, it is challenging to put action behind these words. To be bearers of God's love is to make choices that reflect this love. Good decisions acted upon bear rich fruit. To walk the Christian way, is to make a promise and keep it. Christians cannot say one thing and do another. They cannot believe in something and vote against it. They should prudently speak up and be not afraid to address the social ills that lead people to sin. With help from the Holy Spirit, Christians stand their ground and are not concerned about being politically correct. To live in the light of divine truth is to be a channel of authentic love.

> Jesus calls us; o'er the tumult
> Of our life's wild, restless sea
> Day by day his clear voice soundeth,
> Saying "Christian, follow me!"
>
> As of old, Saint Andrew heard it
> By the Galilean lake,
> Turned from home and toil and kindred,
> Leaving all for his dear sake.

Discipleship: Following Jesus

> Jesus calls us from the worship
> Of the vain world's golden store;
> From each idol that would keep us,
> Saying, "Christian, love me more."
>
> In our joys and in our sorrows,
> Days of toil and hours of ease,
> Still he calls, in cares and pleasures,
> "Christian, love me more than these."
>
> Jesus calls us! By thy mercies,
> Savior, make us hear thy call,
> Give our hearts to thine obedience,
> Serve and love thee best of all.
>
> ~Cecil Francis Alexander
> (1823–1895)

A Catholic who previously had been attending Mass regularly, suddenly stopped going. After a few weeks, the priest decided to visit him. It was a chilly evening. The priest found the man at home, alone, sitting before a blazing fire. Guessing the reason for the priest's visit, the man welcomed him, led him to a comfortable chair near the fireplace and waited. The priest made himself at home but said nothing. In the silence, he contemplated the flames around the burning logs. After some minutes, the priest took the fire tongs, carefully picked up a brightly burning ember and placed it to one side of the hearth. Without speaking, he returned to his chair. The host watched all this in silence. The one lone ember's flame flickered and then diminished until its fire was no more. Soon the ember was dead and cold. Not a word had been spoken since the initial greeting. The priest glanced at his watch and realized it was time to leave. He stood up, picked up the cold, dead ember and placed it back in the middle of the fire. Immediately it began to glow, once more with the light and warmth of the burning coals around it. As the priest reached the door to leave, his host said, "Thank you so much for your visit and especially for the fiery homily. I shall be back in church next Sunday."

To Be Channels of Grace

To grow as Jesus' disciple is to deepen our friendship with him. An external manifestation of this growth is a greater nurturing and protecting of that which is sacred, most importantly the sanctity of all human life. The primary way to live discipleship is gentle interaction with others. John Vianney said, "A young village girl told me, 'When I am about to talk to anyone, I picture to myself Jesus Christ and how gracious and friendly he was to everyone.'" Without Christians being aware of it, their presence should positively affect those around them. A calm demeanor unites and uplifts others. Three things echo in the mind: The first is to be kind, the second is to be kind and the third is to be kind. John Vianney continues: "We love God truly in so far as, when finding ourselves with people who differ from us, we behave graciously to them, speak charitably of them, are willing to meet them again, and to do them a kindness."

Many people are spiritually deaf to God's truth. The Dominican, Catherine of Siena, advises us: "The way to win people's hearts is through peace and love." Because Christians have a deep concern for the salvation of souls, they are kind, firm, clear and direct when trying to help change erroneous ways of thinking. They desire to warm cold hearts with beams of Christ's light. Chromatius of Aquileia said: "Since he is the Sun of Justice, he fittingly calls his disciples the light of the world. For through them, as through shining rays, he has poured out the light of the knowledge of himself upon the entire world. For by manifesting the light of truth, they have dispelled the darkness of error from the hearts of men."

Basking in the light of God's truth, beauty, and goodness endows Christian disciples with a quiet and peaceful heart. The heart is the refuge for prayer, the highest and deepest of the communication arts. Prayer is a launch into the broad ocean of the eternal where there is freedom to commune with the One who always was, is and will be. No passing ship in the night, God is the anchor beneath a boat that keeps passengers tethered to all that is right, good, and just. All things on earth's shore will eventually pass away. On the wide blue ocean, there is nothing more important than holiness and the salvation of souls. In prayer, the storms of earthly cares and fears are reduced to minor squalls. When earthly cares are placed with confidence in God's hands, our thoughts rise above the turbulence of this life to the placid seas of eternity.

Prayer is so vital that without it our existence can spiral downward toward a complete spiritual death. For the next level of prayer to develop, adequate time must be spent in prayer each day. The level of prayer is determined by how well a Christian lives the gospel outside of prayer. Prayer imparts the nutrition and energy necessary to remain spiritually alive and alert to what is going on in society.

Johann Arnold keeps the eyes in focus: "In the face of the strain of tasks beyond our strength, we must turn inward to the Source of strength. If we measure our human strength against the work we see immediately ahead, we shall feel hopeless, and if we tackle it in that strength, we shall be frustrated. . . . There is no healthier lesson we can learn than our own limitations, provided this is accompanied by the resignation of our own strength and reliance on the strength of God. The wheel of life will fly apart unless it is spoked to the Center."

A Contemporary Service of Discipleship

Mabel said only one word the day I met her. It was my first time volunteering at the nursing home. I had taken her on a wheelchair walk through the gardens and, as we stopped to admire the flowers and the birds, I asked Mabel questions and offered a few thoughts of my own. But she said nothing in return. Her only response was a tiny smile that emerged when I picked her a purple petunia.

After we finished our nature tour, we headed inside for the 11:30 Mass at the chapel of this Catholic nursing home. Mabel remained perfectly still until the priest came to give her Holy Communion. At that holy moment, a clear "Amen" rang out of her otherwise silent mouth.

A few days later, I came back for another visit. As I was greeting the residents in the lounge, I noticed Mabel sitting by the window. I walked over and knelt at her side, then took her hand in mine. I looked into her eyes and saw tears trying to escape. Since I now knew she could speak, I asked her what was wrong. To my surprise, she answered.

Quietly, as the first tear was tracing its course down her wrinkled cheek, Mable said, "I want to die. There's nothing left anymore. It's empty." Now it was my turn to be silent.

I searched my heart for a response while my mind raced with suggestions. All of these seemed trite in the face of pain so deep. Soon enough, Mabel spoke again. "I wanted to be so brave," she whispered.

This hit me hard. I didn't have much information, but it was clear that Mabel was not a whiner with a low discomfort threshold. She was a woman of faith and integrity who had intended to face life's challenges with courage and perseverance. But now she was suffering from the greatest of all trials: despair. I reminded Mabel that Jesus also felt abandoned, and that we are never alone in our sorrows. But I knew that it wasn't the time for a theological exposition on the Christian understanding of suffering. Instead of talking about Christianity, I needed to bring Christ to Mabel right then and there. I silently prayed that Jesus would touch her through my hands and that he would love her through my smile. I stayed next to her, holding her hand and drying her tears.

And when 11:30 came around, I was able to take Mabel to literally touch Jesus himself. I prayed for her, asking Jesus to fill Mabel's heart with hope. I believe he answered that prayer. At the end of Mass, Mabel stretched out her arm, took my hand in hers, looked me right in the eye and, smiling said, "God bless you."[1]

A disciple of Jesus does not always walk down a primrose lane. Freezing weather and ice on the trail come to all. This is a fact of the spiritual life. Current trends in society oppose serious faith. Jesus said, "Whoever refuses to take up his cross and follow me cannot be my disciple." Following the way of Jesus will, at times, mean pain. It is only when the rubber of love meets the road of pain that love becomes true. Jesus is near his followers in the "I don't know" times of life. He is close even when his presence is not felt. Roger of Taize advises: "Commit everything to him with the heart of a child. Abandon yourself to him. Entrust to him all that goes against your heart or upsets your plans; pray for your opponent. And sometimes even go so far as to cry out in your pain, when trials abound. . . . Entrust to him now and always whatever disturbs and torments you. And keep silent in his presence."

True followers of Jesus, are called to be more open and loving toward others, and therefore are vulnerable to rejection, suspicion or ridicule. The fresh breezes of hope and faith can change to hot winds of discouragement and doubt. To be alone in a godless society can be frightening. Temptations assault, courage diminishes, praying and caring seem ineffective. It is easy to imagine the terror that Mary and Joseph must have felt when they realized Jesus was not with them and they hurried back to Jerusalem to look for him. Sometimes Jesus seems lost to us. Mary and Joseph found Jesus and so

---

1. Gina Giambrone, *National Catholic Register*, February 25, 2007.

can we. When things get unbearable we tell Jesus about our troubles. We sit in silence and let him love us until inner peace is restored. Through Jesus, our difficulties are transformed and then, they may even be of use to others.

Into the Unknown

To be a disciple of Jesus is to be relatively comfortable with contradiction. The faith of mature disciples is rooted in opposites. The first shall be last. We are in the world but not of it. We are enriched through deprivation, and understand by not understanding. When our lives are more simple they are more profound. Our prayers for enlightenment leave us in the dark. We cannot find our true selves until we find ourselves in Christ. Jesus seems hidden, yet he is most near. The Dominican, Meister Eckhart, counsels: "Even if you cannot conceive of yourself as near to God, you should still regard God as near to you." So, all this isn't frightening, rather it is awe inspiring. Discipleship takes us beyond what we can grasp. Therefore, we relax in the mysterious. Because God is hidden, we can only see him through a glass darkly. At best, God is seen only in shadows. John Henry Newman tells us we cannot bring these shadows together, nor are they all present at once. The image of God is "broken into numberless, partial aspects, independent each of each." Wandering in the mists eventually leads toward a deep longing for God.

Jesus is God's son. However, he emptied himself, assumed the conditions of a slave, and died on the cross. Jesus moved, as Karl Barth observed: "From the heights to the depths, from victory to defeat, from riches to poverty, from triumph to suffering, from life to death." He did not give to others from a privileged position. He went to them and lived among them.

Jesus identified with people in pain by revealing in powerlessness the limitlessness of God's love. In his role as servant, Jesus manifested his divinity. God the Father is known through Jesus the servant. He did not come to rule but to serve. God the Father became better known through Jesus' humble service. Nothing is small in the service of God. If disciples truly love Jesus, they are open to serving him each in their own way, according to their abilities and temperaments.

Disciples need not shout about their faith, or perform big, showy acts of charity. Little ministries can be quite effective. Giving someone a holy card, religious medal or Sacred Heart badge may ignite or intensify their flame of faith. Our discipleship should demonstrate that life would not make sense if Jesus did not exist. True stability is in Jesus. He is the fixed point in ever-changing work and world situations. Teresa of Calcutta said:

> We must not drift away from the humble works because these are the works nobody will do. It is never too small. We are so small and we look at things in a small way. But God, being Almighty, sees everything great. Therefore, even if you write a letter for a blind man or you just go and listen, or you take the mail for him, or you visit somebody, or bring a flower to somebody—small things— or wash clothes for somebody, or clean the house—very humble work—that is where you and I must be. For there are many people who can do big things. But there are very few people who will do the small things.[2]

The type of work done is not important. What is important is to always be faithful to Jesus and his gospel. Oscar Romero wrote these words regarding being disciples of Christ:

> We accomplish in our lifetime only a tiny fraction of the magnificent enterprise that is God's work. Nothing we do is complete, which is another way of saying that the kingdom always lies beyond us. No statement says all that could be said. No prayer fully expresses our faith. No confession brings perfection, no pastoral visit brings wholeness. No program accomplishes the Church's mission. No set of goals and objectives includes everything. This is what we are about. We plant the seeds that one day will grow. We water seeds already planted, knowing that they hold future promise. We lay foundations that will need further development. We provide yeast that produces effects far beyond our capabilities. We cannot do everything, and there is a sense of liberation in realizing that. This enables us to do something, and do it very well. It may be incomplete, but it is a beginning, a step along the way, an opportunity for the Lord's grace to enter and do the rest. We may never see the end results, but that is the difference between the master builder and the worker.[3]

And so we pray,

> Lord Jesus, I give you my hands to do your work; I give you my feet to go your way; I give you my eyes to see as you do; I give you my tongue to speak your words; I give you my mind that you may think in me; I give you my spirit that you may pray in me; Above

---

2. Mother Teresa, *Love: A Fruit Always in Season*.
3. See "Prophets of a Future Not Our Own," at http://www.usccb.org.

all I give you my heart that you may love in me, your Father and all mankind. I give you my whole self, that you may grow in me, so that it is you, Lord Jesus, who lives and works and prays in me. (The Grail)[4]

Weavers of Peace

Peace has a variety of meanings in Hebrew Scriptures. The *Our Sunday Visitor's Catholic Encyclopedia* tells us that peace can stem from the concept of being complete. One's strength is great when complete (Job 9:4), the temple is in good repair when it is complete (1 Kgs 9:25), peace expresses the concept of a completed financial exchange (Exod 21:34) or a vow fulfilled (Ps 50:14). Sometimes peace is identified with good health (Ps 38:4), that which exists between good friends (Ps 41:10, etc.), or the contents of a treaty between allied nations (Josh 9:15, etc.). In the Christian Scriptures, peace is often combined with grace, and is used in the opening lines of a message or letter. Paul's words "Grace be to you and peace from God our Father and the Lord Jesus Christ" are in his letters to the Corinthians, Galatians, Ephesians, Philippians, and Colossians. Peace also indicated an absence of strife (Luke 11:21). The cross of Christ broke the grip of sin, the source of strife because sin separates us from God and his peace.

Peace is so very precious. It comes from God, resides in the human heart and is made manifest by a right and well-ordered life. Living in God's presence and doing his will is striving for holiness. In other words, to want what is right, and strive toward what is good. The wanting and the striving are most important because this is a constant attempt to be united to God's presence and to be attentive to God's graces. Peace is a benevolence that promotes the dignity of every person, helps justice and freedom to prevail, and helps responsibly and respect prevail in commerce. There is no lasting peace without God. The foundress of the Benedictine Sisters of Jesus Crucified, Mere Marie des Douleurs, wrote:

> True peace, that which is "beyond all knowledge" and which Christ came to bring to the earth, is the result of the deep harmony of our whole being with God, a resting of our whole being in the

4. The Grail is a secular institute for lay women based in England. A secular institute is an organization of individuals who are consecrated persons. They profess the evangelical counsels of poverty, chastity and obedience, and are dedicated to the work of the institute. The Grail includes women who live in residence at their institute or in their own homes. They also have a collaborators' section.

will of the Father. If we are not self seeking we are at peace, we are held fast in the depths of ourselves and 'moored' in God, a bit like a ship which, in spite of the storm, remains where it is, even though waves break against it, because it has dropped anchor. We can suffer from the waves of temptations and yet be at peace, if we seek God alone.[5]

Disciples weave threads of the peace of Christ into the fabric of society. Like seasoned weavers of fine fabric, this call is to weave strong threads of peace into a worn and torn cloth. These threads of peace need to hold stronger than patchwork. How can peace weavers be authentic? This well-known advice is attributed to Francis of Assisi:

Lord, make me an instrument of your peace. Where there is hatred, let me sow love; where there is injury, pardon; where there is doubt, faith; where there is despair, hope; where there is darkness, light; where there is sadness, joy. Oh, Divine Master, grant that I may not so much seek to be consoled, as to console; to be understood as to understand; to be loved, as to love. For it is in giving that we receive; It is in pardoning that we are pardoned; It is in dying that we are born to eternal life.

Inner Peace

Each person can participate in these actions. No matter how large or small the contribution, every little bit helps to spread peace. However, before moving into action there is something that must be present inside: interior peace. A person cannot give what he or she does not have. Inner peace is based on Christ's peace, the deepest peace known to humanity. "The Christian has a deep, silent, hidden peace, which the world sees not, like some well in a retired and shady place," wrote John Henry Newman. Jesus' peace passes all understanding, has no end to its depth and keeps an individual in touch with what is most real in his or her life. Interior peace also keeps a person sane in negative and positive situations. When the peace of Christ is passed on to others, it is not lost in the giving. Rather it increases in an

---

5. From *Magnificat*, a liturgical and devotional monthly magazine, edited by Father Peter John Cameron, OP (New York, date unknown). In 1930, Mere Marie des Douleurs (1902–1983) founded the Benedictine Sisters of Jesus Crucified, in France. They are an international monastic congregation of contemplative Benedictine religious sisters. Their particular gift is to make monastic life possible for women who might not normally be admitted to a monastery due to a physical impediment.

individual as he or she gives it away. It brings out extraordinary love and goodness because followers of Christ are the ones who embody the presence of Christ in their families and communities.

Can dreams of peace turn into programs of action for peace? Only if that peace comes from God. God's peace is the foundation for peace in society, politics and economics. The peace of Christ is deeper than peace born out of intellects, ideas, relationships or programs. A peace that is of one's own liking isn't really peace. Peace begins in God, flows through an individual and into humanity through programs, laws, declarations or treaties that are based on the teachings of Jesus. Through his suffering and death, Jesus broke the chains of sin that bound humanity. Since then humanity receives new life from Jesus and benefits from an eternal friendship with God. The Catechism of the Catholic Church tells us:

> Respect for and development of human life require peace. Peace is not merely the absence of war, and it is not limited to maintaining a balance of powers between adversaries. Peace cannot be attained on earth without safeguarding the goods of persons, free communication among men, respect for the dignity of persons and peoples, and the assiduous practice of fraternity. Peace is "the tranquility of order." Peace is the work of justice and the effect of charity. Earthly peace is the image and fruit of the peace of Christ, the messianic "Prince of Peace." By the blood of his cross, "in his own person he killed the hostility," he reconciled men with God and made his Church the sacrament of the unity of the human race and of its union with God. "He is our peace." He has declared: "Blessed are the peacemakers." (.CCC 2304–5)

The peace of Christ is like warmth and light from an everlasting sun in which humankind can bask in good times and in bad. His peace is priceless, measureless and always available. It is up to the individual to stay connected with it, by pondering it in quiet times and living it in daily activities. Christ's peace is like an invisible force, which slows Christians down and helps them in doing good, building trust, having courage and making the right decisions. Jesus' peace helps maintain an attitude of love and kindness in all situations. John Eudes gives a push forward regarding the peace of Christ: "He belongs to you, but more than that, he longs to be in you, living and ruling in you, as the head lives and rules in the body. He wants his breath to be in your breath, his heart in your heart, and his soul in your soul." It is a beautiful blessing beyond compare to be a disciple of Jesus and bearer of his message. To experience the peace of Christ is to desire it for all humanity. R. Jordan says this well:

> Our wish for the world . . .
> a place where Christ can find a home,
> hearts that love each other,
> lives embraced by heaven's joy,
> helping one another.
> An end to terror, war and want,
> forgiveness of the past,
> children safe from every harm . . .
> and peace on earth at last.

Inner peace, the peace of Christ, is like the calm in the eye of a hurricane. Sometimes troubles whirl around the periphery, but there is tranquility at the center. If lies or rumors are being spread about a Christian, he or she may be sad or hurt, but not unduly so because inner peace offers solace within its sturdy refuge. Jesus facilitates being at peace while being tempted, anxious or afraid. This peace never leaves as long as prayer fortifies it. Prayer softens hearts so that phrases like "I don't want to see, speak or forgive this person" are not part of one's vocabulary. The more a Christian grows in friendship with Jesus the deeper peace will be. The person who cultivates inner peace wants to pray better and pray more. Prayer is the foundation of peace. It makes a Christian beautiful on the inside because he or she is joined with him who is most beautiful. As we disciples walk along the way, let us be good pray-ers, and good peacemakers, in, with and through Jesus.

"Jesu, Nostra Redemptio"[6]

> O Jesus, Savior, Lord of all;
> What mind would ever span
> The measure of your mighty love,
> O Savior, Son of man?
>
> What loving mercy held your heart
> That you should bear our sin?

---

6. Translated by Ralph Wright, OSB, St. Louis, Missouri.

Discipleship: Following Jesus

    Should let yourself be crushed by death
        That our life might begin?

    You broke the power of sin and death,
        Your tore the gateway wide;
    And all who welcomed you were led
        Back to the Father's side.

    May this same love surround us now
        To free us from all harm,
    That we may soon meet face to face
        Within our Father's home.

    O Jesus, be our joy this day,
        Our comfort in this place;
    May this your risen life be ours
        That we may know your peace.

Prayer: Our Privilege and Our Gift

IN 1819, JOSEPH SCRIVEN was born in Ireland. He was raised by well-to-do parents and graduated from Trinity College in Dublin. Happily engaged to be married, his fiancée drowned the night before their wedding. This had a profound effect on Joseph. When he was twenty-five, he moved to Canada, and was known to be a bit odd because he began to take Jesus' Sermon on the Mount very seriously. He believed it in the depths of his heart and lived it in the days of his life. He gave freely of his few possessions, even to the clothes he wore, and was known for his kindness. He walked the streets with his sawhorse and saw, where he cut wood and did menial jobs for the widows, the sick and others who could not afford to pay him. He never refused help to anyone who needed assistance.

Joseph was poor, so he could not visit his mother in Ireland, when she became very ill. Instead, he sent her a comforting letter and enclosed a poem he wrote called "Pray without Ceasing." The simple poem came from his heart. It gave his mother strength and support. Joseph never intended that his poem be published. He passed away in an accidental drowning in 1896. Charles Converse set his poem to music. It became one of the most beloved hymns in Christendom:

> What a friend we have in Jesus, all our sins and griefs to bear.
> What a privilege to carry everything to God in prayer.
> O what peace we often forfeit. O what needless pain we bear.
> All because we do not carry everything to God in prayer.
>
> Have we trials and temptations? Is there trouble anywhere?
> We should never be discouraged: Take it to the Lord in prayer.

Prayer: Our Privilege and Our Gift

> Can we find a friend so faithful, who will all our sorrows share?
> Jesus knows our every weakness. Take it to the Lord in prayer.
>
> Are we weak and heavy laden, cumbered with a load of care?
> Precious Saviour, still our refuge: Take it to the Lord in prayer.
> Do thy friends despise, forsake thee? Take it to the Lord in prayer.
> In his arms he'll take and shield thee. Thou will find a solace there.

Prayer is the foundation for a well-lived life of holiness. A conscientious discipline of prayer prevents a soul from shriveling and keeps a body moving forward. It provides energy for work and help for decisions. No matter how busy Christians may be, they pray because prayer is their lifeline to God. Fidelity to prayer is strong, regardless of moods, because prayer is the heartbeat of a sound spiritual life. It fosters growth in Christ and nourishes the soul. Prayer generates the energy needed to go on with life.

Prayer reinforces a connection with those in the heavenly realm, as well as with all of us and all that is good on earth. There is no true Christian life without prayer. Thomas Fuller tells us, "A good prayer, though often used, is still fresh and fair in the eyes and ears of heaven." Prayer is God's gift because it unites us who are finite to him who is infinite. This precious gift sustains the faith that flowers into the many blossoms of God's love which results in being good and doing good on earth, and truly believing in heaven.

In time, prayer becomes a blessed routine, independent of feelings because it infuses love and grace into the day and sustains perseverance and hope into the years. The practice of daily prayer helps maintain a gentle rhythm that pulses through the solemnities, ordinary ferias, and long plateaus in life. Therefore, it is beloved in the heart. Prayer sustains a God-centered vision that looks ahead toward something better than what is. Yet, daily prayer is not easy. Often prayer is difficult, dull, energy draining or void of comforts. However, perseverance prevails even when there are no spiritual highs or enthusiasm for holiness. We plod along in prayer because we know it is our lifeline.

Basil Hume wrote these comforting words:

> I went on gazing out of the window. Then suddenly the fog lifted. It began to waft away. I now saw what the fog had hidden, a lovely view of the garden. The colors of the flowers seemed to dance before my eyes, and their beauty sent messages to my mind to express delight in what I saw.... It is often thus in prayer. So often

words and thoughts are quite hopeless, for there is fog in my mind, or at least there seems to be. But stick at it, say the words, try to think. Don't walk away. Suddenly the fog will lift. The words or the thoughts will begin to send their messages to mind and heart. Dry and cold before, they now come to life. . . . I went on gazing out of the window, but alas, the fog came down again, and hid the garden from my view. . . . It is like that in the spiritual life, moments of delight, followed by dryness and coldness. But never walk away. Go on praying, and wait for the fog to lift again or even one day to go away altogether.[1]

As Hume suggests, a Christian needs to keep praying even when he or she feels nothing, sees nothing, or receives nothing. At these times, prayer is most pleasing to God. To love God is to pray, no matter what the season or the day.

Gift from the Heart

An old Hebrew saying asks, "What is the service of the heart?" and answers, "It is prayer." To receive a novena of Masses, or a spiritual bouquet of prayers, is a most beautiful and time-honored gift. We give the gift of prayer when we sincerely pray from our heart. We say a daily rosary for a wayward loved one, a novena for a special intention, or recite the Litany of the Holy Name for our favorite priest or for all priests. There are so many variations of prayer from the heart: a sigh of adoration, a cry for help, a song of delight, a word of thanks, a gesture of kindness, an act of contrition, a sweet peace, a reflection on Jesus' words or an act of reparation for those who do not love him. We can say these prayers anytime and anywhere, and each kind of prayer has its own fruits of grace.

It is lovely and peaceful to sit quietly, gaze at the beauty of Jesus and rest in his love. A young girl came out of her church alone. Her aunt asked her, "Where were you?" "In church," said the girl. "What were you doing in church on such a beautiful spring day?" the aunt gently asked. "Praying," said the child. "What were you praying for?" "Nothing," said the girl, "I just loved God." Prayer helps quench the thirst for the fullness of love, beauty

---

1. "The Living Spirit," a regular column of about five quotes that is in *The Tablet*, an international weekly review published in London (date unknown). Basil Hume was an English Benedictine, a monk and priest of Ampleforth Abbey, where he served as abbot for thirteen years. In 1976 he was appointed as Archbishop of Westminster and later was made a cardinal. He died in 1999.

and truth and can be spontaneous or formal, as simple as a loving sigh or as profound as the Eucharistic Sacrifice. Therese of Lisieux said, "Prayer means a launching out of the heart toward God, it means lifting up one's eyes, quite simply, to heaven, a cry of grateful love, from the crest of joy or the trough of despair; it's a vast, supernatural force that opens out my heart and binds me close to Jesus." Because there are many ways to pray we choose what we think is best for us, relax and let God lead us toward his land of mystery.

Prayer shows us how fragmented humankind would be without God, and unites humans with the wholeness of God. Prayer must be looked at differently than other routine actions. More than simply a daily activity, it is the substance from which individuals mature spiritually. Through prayer, we no longer see God only as a benevolent being who gives goodies, heals or gets people out of trouble. God is the object of our prayer, and we pray because it is right and just to do so. Teresa of Avila wrote that we must love the God of consolations, rather than the consolations of God.

The most natural part of the day should be prayer: A communion of love with God. Prayer enfolds in God's love and unfolds in service to others. Like a bubbling spring, prayer is the source for streams of service that let the waters of God's love flow into society. We draw nearer to him and bring those for whom we pray closer to him even though they may not realize it. When prayer is based on what we give rather than what we receive, and how we love rather than what we think, it becomes the center of the foundation on which we build our lives rather than an isolated part of the framework of our lives. Prayer is lived to the extent that action is given to good intentions. Assiduous prayer is manifest by a Christ-like understanding of who a person is. When we see with light from God's grace, the world begins to be transformed because we are transformed. Teresa of Calcutta was extremely aware of dirty, grimy slums and down-trodden humanity. She saw violence and anger as the result of hurt and pain in people's souls. She also saw Christ within each person she met. Father Solanus Casey would answer his monastery door with the firm conviction that any person who knocked on it was either an angel or a saint. He held on to this belief in the midst of questions that would drive anyone else to distraction. We begin to learn the secret of sanctity when small irritants and large adversities become conduits that take us from superficial difficulties and little deaths to limitless life with God in a reality that does not die. We step back from what we perceive through our senses and strive to see with the eyes of Christ. And we spend time in reflective prayer. It is very beautiful when prayer passes from swimming in the water of petitions to floating in the ocean of God's mercy. Things that hurt are easier to bear when we enter into God's presence in our souls and absorb his wisdom in silence. Sometimes disappointments can be God's protective wings. Amid pain and poverty, in whatever form they take, God is the greatest refuge.

Listening Heart

Prayer is less a work of mental exercise than it is a rest in God's love. In his book *Creative Prayer*, Metropolitan Anthony Bloom[2] relates the following story:

> I remember one of the first people who came to me for advice when I was ordained was an old lady who said: "Father, I have been praying almost unceasingly for fourteen years, and I have never had any sense of God's presence." "So," I said, "Did you give him a chance to put in a word?" "Oh well," she said, "No, I have been talking to him all the time, because is not that prayer?" I said, "No, I do not think it is, and what I suggest is that you should set apart fifteen minutes a day, sit and just knit before the face of God." And so she did. What was the result? Quite soon she came again and said: "It is extraordinary, when I pray to God, in other words, when I talk to him, I feel nothing, but when I sit quietly, face to face with him, then I feel wrapped in his presence." You will never be able to pray to God really and from all your heart unless you learn to keep silent and rejoice in the miracle of his presence, or if you prefer, of your being face to face with him although you do not see him.

God should be so much a part of our lives that silence with him is a refuge and spontaneous chats with him are commonplace. When we are tired, we ask God to be near us. We tell him about the little things that have happened during the day, especially our fears, doubts, and sorrows. Nothing may be resolved, but we have shared what concerns us most with

---

2. Metropolitan Anthony Bloom (1914-2003) was best known as a writer, preacher, pastor, spiritual director and broadcaster on prayer and the Christian life. He was a monk, bishop and Metropolitan of the Russian Orthodox diocese of Sourozh in Great Britain and Ireland.

the one who cares for us the most. Francois Fénelon, a seventeenth-century Catholic Frenchman, gives us this good advice about prayer:

> Tell God all that is in your heart, as one unloads one's heart, its pleasures and its pains, to a dear friend. Tell him your troubles, that he may comfort you; tell him your joys, that he may sober them; tell him your longings, that he may purify them; tell him your dislikes, that he may help you to conquer them; talk to him of your temptations, that he may shield you from them; show him the wounds of your heart, that he may heal them; lay bare your indifference to good, your depraved tastes for evil, your instability. Tell him how self love makes you unjust to others, how vanity tempts you to be insincere, how pride disguises you to yourself and others.
>
> If you thus pour out all your weaknesses, needs, troubles, there will be no lack of what to say. You will never exhaust the subject. It is continually being renewed. People who have no secrets from each other never want for subject of conversation. They do not weigh their words, for there is nothing to be held back, neither do they seek for something to say. They talk out of the abundance of the heart, without consideration they say just what they think. Blessed are they who attain to such familiar, unreserved intercourse with God.[3]

A man's daughter had asked the local priest to come and pray with her father. When the priest arrived, he found the man lying in bed with his head propped up on the pillows. An empty chair sat beside his bed. The priest assumed that the old fellow had been informed of his visit. "I guess you were expecting me," he said. "No, who are you?" said the father. The priest told him his name and then remarked, "I saw the empty chair and I thought you knew I was going to show up." "Oh yes, the chair," said the bedridden man, "Would you mind closing the door?" Puzzled the priest shut the door. "I have never told anyone this, not even my daughter," said the man. "But all of my life I have never known how to really pray. At church I used to hear the priest talk about prayer, but it went right over my head. I abandoned any serious attempt at prayer until one day, four years ago, my best friend said to me, 'Johnny, prayer is just a simple matter of having a conversation with Jesus. Here is what I suggest. Sit down in a chair; place an empty chair in front of you, and in faith see

---

3. Fénelon, *Talking with God*. François Fénelon was a French Roman Catholic archbishop, theologian, poet, and writer.

Jesus on the chair. It's not spooky because he promised, 'I will be with you always.' Then just speak to him in the same way you are doing with me right now.' So I tried it, and I've liked it so much that I do it a couple of hours every day. I am careful though. If my daughter saw me talking to an empty chair, she would either have a nervous breakdown or send me off to the funny farm." The priest was deeply moved by the story and encouraged the old man to continue on the journey. Then he anointed him and returned to the church.

Two nights later, the daughter called to tell the priest that her daddy had died that afternoon. "Did he die in peace?" he asked. "Yes, when I left the house at about two o'clock, he called me over to his bedside, told me he loved me and kissed me on the cheek. When I got back from the store an hour later, I found him dead. But there was something strange about his death. Apparently, just before daddy died, he leaned over and rested his head on the chair beside the bed. What do you make of that?" The priest wiped a tear from his eye and said: "I wish we could all go like that."

Cautions

To try to pray beyond one's level of spiritual development can do more harm than good. Someone said we should pray as we can, not as we can't. To pretend to be holy will not do. To recite continual aspirations by rote can bring about a nervous disorder or obsession. To be overly involved in prayer may encourage a loss of touch with reality, a trance, or false spirituality. There are certain inner dynamics that may appear very pious but do not have a thing to do with God. Prayer should be courteous because God is a gentleman. Demanding prayers that tell God to do this or not to do that, or nonsensical prayers, or prayers with excessive flowery words, are prayers badly said. Conversely, to thank God for things not to one's liking shows spiritual strength.

> Lord, day after day I've thanked you
> for saying yes.
> But when have I genuinely thanked
> you for saying no?
>
> Yet I shudder to think
> of the possible smears

Prayer: Our Privilege and Our Gift

> The cumulative blots on my life
> Had you not been sufficiently wise
> to say an unalterable no.
>
> So thank you for saying no
> When my want list for things
> Far exceeded my longing for you.
> When I asked for a stone
> foolishly certain I asked for bread
> Thank you for saying no
>
> To my petulant "Just this time Lord?"
> Thank you for saying no
> To senseless excuses
> selfish motives
> dangerous diversions.
>
> Thank you for saying no
> When the temptation that enticed me
> Would have bound me beyond escape.
>
> Thank you for saying no
> When I asked you to leave me alone.
>
> Above all thank you for saying no
> When in anguish I asked
> "If I give you all else
> may I keep this?"
>
> Lord, my awe increases
> When I see the wisdom
> of your divine no.
>
> ~Ruth Harms Calkin
> "Tell Me Again Lord, I Forget"

    Variety in daily time and place is not the spice of prayer. Neither is vibrant energy. Burning intensity or joyful affection are not indicators of good prayer. These are secondary and accidental to the primary purpose of prayer which is presence and communion with God in faith.

Prayer may bring surprises. Often individuals pray best when they don't realize they are praying. John of the Cross suggested that many people pray intensely but don't realize they are praying. Others place a high value on their prayer, which is little more than nonexistent. The "high value" to which he refers are those emotional highs that make us feel good. If we find prayer consoling it is not necessarily a sign that our prayer is pleasing to God. If we experience dryness or distractions in prayer, it does not mean that God is displeased with us. Solace makes it easier to pray, but a more heroic prayer has no rewards and requires more effort and love from us. Feeling good is a nice reward of prayer for us, but the essence of prayer is to pray to God because he is who he is and we want to know him better. Our prayer is an act of will and we pray when we are up or down, in good and bad times, in sunshine and rain. We pray because we love God, and our love is constant even when we don't feel it, or when we mumble disjointed prayers that cannot find appropriate words or cohesive thoughts. Teresa of Avila consoles us: "Love consists not in the extent of our happiness, but in the firmness of our determination to try to please God in everything." When our prayer feels as dry as desert dust, we can offer it to God as a gift of love.

Prayer must not descend into superstition or magic, or be an escape from our responsibilities. God intervenes, but we must do our part. He gave us intelligence and free will. Usually God doesn't give supernatural assistance if we can attain something by our own efforts. If we have been healed by medication, surgery or other treatments, we have seen how God works through others. When human resources are available, they must be utilized.

It is of utmost importance to stick with the daily habit of prayer in spite of distractions. Distractions are most common. Prayer would not be prayer without them. As soon as we are aware of a distraction, it should take us back to prayer. One of the stories Fulton Sheen liked to tell was about St. Bernard. He was horseback riding with a friend of his, and the friend said to him, "I never have a distraction during prayer." Bernard said, "I have many." And Bernard then said, "Very well, you get off your horse, and if you can say the Our Father without a single distraction, I will give you my horse." So this friend got off his horse, and began to recite the Our

Father. When he got to the words "Give us this day our...," he stopped and said to Bernard, "Can I have the saddle, too?"

Learning the sacred art of prayer continues throughout life. It has so many different facets. John Cassian tells us:

> It is certain moreover, that nobody is ever able to keep praying in the same way. A person prays in one manner when cheerful, in another when weighed down by sadness or a sense of hopelessness. When one is flourishing spiritually, prayer is different from when one is oppressed by the extent of one's struggles. One prays in this manner when seeking pardon for sins, and in another when asking for a particular grace or virtue or the elimination of a particular vice. Sometimes prayer is conditioned by compunction, occasioned by the thought of hell and desire for the good things to come. A person prays in one manner when in dangerous straits and in another when enjoying quiet and security. Prayer is sometimes illuminated by the revelation of heavenly mysteries, but at other times one is forced to be content with the sterile practice of virtue and the experience of aridity.[4]

To pray always does not mean a continuous verbal or mental recital of memorized words. Rather, it is a beautiful ideal for which to strive: being responsive to the presence of God within and around everyone. We only find the presence of God around us after we have discovered the presence of God within us. To pray always is to focus on what is most real. Through grace, the Triune God is revealed slowly, gently and reverently, in the here and now of each day. Unceasing prayer means abiding in the Triune God who resides in the heart. To dwell on this truth is to mature in prayer.

Augustine of Hippo adds another perspective to praying always. He says, "If you want to pray without ceasing, never cease to long for God. The continuation of your longing is the continuation of your prayer; and if you cease to long for him, this prayer will also cease."

Ora et Labora

John Paul II said, "God loves for us to pray to him and he very much dislikes our making prayer an excuse for neglecting the effort of good works." Prayer cannot be an excuse to get out of doing work. Neither can work be

---

4. Quoted in Casey, *Strangers to the City*. John Cassian was a Christian monk and theologian known in both the Western and Eastern Churches for his mystical writings.

a substitute for prayer. Ora et labora, prayer and work, are both good and necessary. However, prayer has a higher importance. Work is temporary, done for a time during one's earthly life which will come to an end. Prayer sustains a relationship with the all holy immortal God and a life that will last forever in heaven. If daily priorities are in good order, prayer will be at the top of the list. Daily prayer is of primary importance because it helps to realize the importance of God in daily duties, responsibilities, problems and trials. By daily practice of the art of prayer, somehow everything that needs to be done gets done, and eventually problems are resolved. Good pray-ers are not slackers or procrastinators. It is a singular grace to persevere in prayer no matter what happens.

The "it's all about me" mentality is so common in today's society. Prayer changes this mindset because actually "it's all about Jesus." This isn't the "nice" Jesus who loves me just the way I am, especially if I am content in my sins, but the challenging Jesus who loves me infinitely and tells me to "sin no more." Deep prayer is a gift from God to us and reveals that I am a sinner in need of conversion no matter how good I look to others. Deep prayer reinforces the desire to be a saint, which can be defined as a Christian who keeps on trying. Eric Hoffer said: "Many of the insights of the saint stem from his experiences as a sinner." For Christians, life is a struggle against sin. Because sin offends God, and dehumanizes and diminishes society, it should never be taken lightly or used as a topic for silly jokes. An individual chooses to sin, and every personal sin has a social consequence. One feature of moving closer to the light of Christ is seeing how often we sin. Every person on earth is a sinner. There is an old prayer said before a crucifix that keeps this sinner status at the forefront:

> Sweet Jesus, for how many ages hast thou hung upon thy Cross, and still men pass thee by and regard thee not, except to pierce anew thy Sacred Heart. How often have I passed thee by, heedless of thy great sorrow, thy many wounds, thy infinite love! How often have I stood before thee, not to comfort and console thee, but to add to thy sorrow, to deepen thy wounds, to scorn thy love. Thou hast stretched forth thy hands to comfort me, to raise me up, and I have taken those hands that might have struck me into hell and have bent them back on the Cross and nailed them there, rigid and helpless. Yet I have but succeeded in engraving my name on thy palms forever! Thou hast loved me with an infinite love and I have taken advantage of that love to sin the more against thee; yet my ingratitude has but pierced thy Sacred Heart and forth upon me has flowed thy Precious Blood. O sweet Jesus, let thy Blood

be upon me, not for a curse, but for a blessing. Lamb of God, who takest away the sins of the world, have mercy on me! Amen.

"Holy Mary, Mother of God, pray for us sinners. . . ." It is comforting to dwell upon the most beloved prayer in the Catholic world. Sung at weddings, said at funerals, the Hail Mary is a classic.

> The Hail Mary has its own rhythm, which again is universal in its ability to commune with heaven and to communicate with others. . . . Like any song, it is repeated over and over again in a rhymed refrain, all for the purpose of delighting the heart and lifting the soul out of the mundane, into the world of the spirit. Only the unthinking and insensitive can knock this rhythm of the heavens. . . . Yes, indeed, the Hail Mary falls like a sound of the other world on this vale of tears. . . . We are talking about a given song, a heaven sent sound. St Dominic heard a voice from heaven saying: "Dominic, my son, be of good courage. Remember that the earth was dry and barren until watered by the dew of the heavenly Ave." . . . Like the rhythm of the rain, the Hail Mary falls like liquid sunshine upon the barren land of our being. We simply expose ourselves to its down pouring upon the hardness of our hearts. There is a sense in which we do not so much say this prayer as listen to the Lord as he speaks to the maid of Nazareth and to the whole world whom she represented on that day of Annunciation. Reason will find its way, but the rhythm and rhyme will prepare a pathway. So, let's not despise the little earthy ways of the rosary that lead to the heavenly highway.[5]

It is easy to experience God in the happy times or in the fleeting successes that come into our days, but not as easy to experience him in the sad events or disappointing setbacks that just as often come into our lives. People of prayer must hear God's call everywhere. He is the goal to whom the eyes of the soul are fixed. There are many ways to walk away from Jesus through sin. However, with the aid of grace, each wandering is quickly met with a return to him. Prayer helps iron out the painful wrinkles in the fabric of life. The grace of God works in difficult times and in hard circumstances. No matter what happens, life will be easier to bear if we persevere in prayer. At the kitchen sink or at the office water cooler, we meet God where we are. It is impossible to understand how he is present in all things. God's actions are too bewildering for our limited scope of understanding. To approach people and circumstances that baffle us with respect and treat them with

---

5. Gabriel Harty, OP, *The Riches of the Rosary*, 7.

reverence is a mark of deep prayer. All things are accepted with trust when we live the love of God.

> Be thou my vision, O Lord of my heart,
> Naught be all else to me, save that thou art;
> Thou my best thought in the day and the night,
> Waking or sleeping, thy presence my light.
>
> Be thou my wisdom, be thou my true word,
> I ever with thee, and thou with me, Lord;
> Thou my great Father, and I thy true son;
> Thou in me dwelling, and I with thee one.
>
> Riches I heed not, nor man's empty praise,
> Thou mine inheritance through all my days;
> Thou, and thou only the first in my heart,
> High King of heaven, my treasure thou art!
>
> High King of heaven, thou heaven's bright sun,
> Grant me its joys after vict'ry is won;
> Christ of my own heart, whatever befall,
> Still be my vision, O Ruler of All.[6]

---

6. Eleanor Henrietta Hull, in *Daily Prayer from the Divine Office*, 604*.

Work: To Serve with Dignity

WHAT IS OUR ULTIMATE purpose in life? Many people think it is to gain money, possessions and success. However, if they want to find life's definitive purpose they need to look deeper. God, the one who loves us more than any human possibly could, knew us before we were conceived. Therefore, our purpose in life must be connected with God. The old Baltimore Catechism asks: Why did God make us? The answer is: To know him, love him and serve him in this world and to be happy with him forever in the next. With the transitory value of earthly things, and the fact that our bodies will not last forever here on earth, this answer makes great good sense.

It is true that we can be reasonably comfortable and happy while here on earth without an eternal focus. But what is more important: comfort or character, popularity or piety, happiness or holiness? Service is a manifestation of holiness. Much of work contains within it a dimension of service. To serve is a sign of love. Service is an important component of work and work is an essential element of life. To be able to work with love and perseverance contributes to a well-balanced life and to the well-being of humankind. According to Gerard Manley Hopkins: "It is not only prayer that gives God glory but work. Smiting on an anvil, sawing a beam, whitewashing a wall, driving horses, sweeping, scouring, everything gives God some glory if being in his grace you do it as your duty. To go to communion worthily gives God great glory, but a man with a dung fork in his hand, a woman with a slop pail, gives him glory too. He is so great that all things give him glory if you mean they should." We all have work tasks that give us the opportunity to develop our gifts for the glory of God and for the common good. Everything we do can become a means by which we deepen our friendship with God.

John Henry Newman wrote these words to ponder:

> God has created me to do him some definite service; He has committed some work to me which he has not committed to another. I have my mission—I may never know it in this life, but I shall be told it in the next. I am a link in a chain, a bond of connection between persons. He has not created me for naught. I shall do good; I shall do his work. I shall be an angel of peace, a preacher of truth in my own place while not intending it, if I do but keep his commandments. Therefore I will trust him. Whatever, wherever I am, I can never be thrown away. If I am in sickness, my sickness may serve him, in perplexity, my perplexity may serve him. He does nothing in vain. He knows what he is about. He may take away my friends; he may throw me among strangers. He may make me feel desolate, make my spirits sink, hide my future from me, still he knows what he is about.[1]

Labors make sense when people understand they were made by God and for God. This is evident in the Christian work ethic. Work tasks permeate the day. There are tasks for the home, on the job, in volunteer situations, educational pursuits and church activities. Christian effectiveness is not measured by what we accomplish or if we are successful. We must persevere in our responsibilities and labors despite their repetitive nature. How we behave as Christians in the marketplace is more important than what we achieve or accomplish. God's love is manifest through us. Musings on God and the world to come put tasks into perspective and give courage to be countercultural. Christians may be unpopular in many quarters because of what they believe. However, the price of not following what is right in the heart is to live that lie in the soul. Those lies can build up and harden people in such a way that they lose the ability to think honestly and follow God's truth. By living what is good and true we encourage others toward what is good and true so that they might become better individuals. This usually does not happen through theological statements, sentimental piety, self-righteous behavior or defense tactics. It is a result of searching for, finding, and disseminating truth by example. It is also a result of honing the ability to make reasoned judgments and have positive conversations about why we carry out activities. Activities can range from being helpful to others to self-serving devices. G. K. Chesterton noted, "The Catholic Church is the only thing which saves a man from the degrading slavery of being a child of his age." Today, there is no voice that champions authentic human freedom and human dignity more than the Catholic Church.

---

1. See "Mission of My Life," at the John Henry Newman Catholic College website.

Meister Eckhart advises us,

> People should not think so much about what they do, but rather should they think upon what they are. If only they themselves were good and their way of life, then their works would give forth a beautiful light. If you yourself are just, then will your work be just. Do not think to found holiness upon doing, holiness must be founded upon being. Works do not make us holy. It is we who must make works holy. For no matter how holy works may be, they do not make us holy because we do them, but in so far as we within ourselves are as we should be, we make holy all that we do, whether it be eating, or sleeping, or waking, or what it may. Those whose nature is not great, no matter what they do, it will be as nothing.[2]

A key to holiness is to recognize God working in all that is around us. God speaks in the most commonplace things, many of which are overlooked. Consider an average twenty-dollar bill. This bill has its history and secrets in its creases or age. It can represent labor, leisure, toil, values, pleasure, payment, joys, degradations, dreams and little deaths. It may have bought flowers for a loved one, liquor, toys for a child, obscene magazines, food through a care agency, a meal for one. A twenty-dollar bill could be used as a source for life or for death, buying something that directs a person to heaven or to hell. An individual can use a twenty-dollar bill for good or ill. Using this money for a good purpose is a sign of living in holiness. Sinful use causes destruction and suffering.

Virtues at Work

To come to know God better is to want to reflect something of his goodness to others. Therefore, virtues must be the foundation for work. To feel compassion for others in difficult circumstances is to want to help them. Bonaventure in his treatise "Bringing Forth Christ" observes: "Anyone who keeps close to a holy man discovers that by seeing him often, listening to his words and witnessing his exemplary behavior, he is set on fire with love of the truth, keeps away from the darkness of sin, and is inflamed by the

---

2. Reinhold, *The Soul Afire*, 95. Meister Eckhart was a thirteenth- to fourteenth-century priest, philosopher, theologian, and mystic who was a member of the Dominican Order. He led a relatively successful academic life and was considered to be an influential orator and preacher.

love of divine light. . . . Seek the company of good people. If you share their company, you will also share their virtue."

Christians come to know virtue by seeking it, learn virtue by practicing it, and live virtuously when the practice becomes habitual. When the challenge of living the virtues takes root, lifestyles are in greater harmony with the gospel. The Christian practice of virtue deepens one's roots in the gospel. This is most necessary because we do not want to be blown away by the ever changing winds of society. However, virtues are not an end in themselves, rather they are a means to an end. If we practice virtue just to feel good about ourselves, then we end up praising ourselves instead of God. In the most virtuous person there is a little vice, and in the vilest of persons there is a little virtue. Every virtue has a corresponding vice. Faith has doubt, hope has despair, love has indifference, justice has corruption and honesty has fraud. Virtue in actions produces good, but virtue can slide down a pole into its opposing vice. False pride can easily be the grease on the pole. A Christian need not talk about her virtuous actions, as such actions speak for themselves. Human nature is exulted when there is the desire to be true in speech, just in judgment, competent in business, and respectful toward all. There is no need to call attention to how good one is.

Holiness is a haunting mystery to pursue, as it is the perfect manifestation of authentic personhood. God alone knows who the holy ones are. In the quest for God, the more Christians are united to God, the more their reverence for virtue increases. Teresa of Avila wrote: "I would never want any prayer that would not make the virtues grow within me." This is a great challenge. A Christian tries to live the virtues in the present yet sometimes with difficulty, because it is not always personally agreeable. When we have a bad day, or are feeling down, we would rather complain. Living virtues can be frustrating, drab and rarely easy. There is a certain amount of blundering, lack of sensitivity and loss of interest. Sometimes the best we can give others is our attention, yet we know that in our attention we feel nothing. However, there is peace. We try to live virtuously with or without good feelings.

Virtues reveal Christians to themselves. Sometimes this is disturbing. To find the true motivations behind behavior can be alarming. Conversely, there is pleasure in finding hidden talents and gifts in ourselves and in others. To become more aware of how greatly God loves people is very consoling. A prayerful instinct develops when there is no concern about the why behind the good things people do. The power of God's love is realized through the power of human virtues. Growing in holiness is striving to be one's best self.

The nobility of holiness shines in living the virtues at all times. Holiness is the greatest need in the workplace because it is the purest reflection of God and an indestructible force for good. Catholics are called to fight against corruption, unfair competition, and harmful business practices, to protect human rights, to set an example of sound ethics and personal integrity, and to know what is right and good and do it. This takes a heap of grace. Catholics should be ever watchful so they do not fall prey to insidious or popular trends that compromise their beliefs. Speculations about what is right and good do not cut it. Virtuous action is the witness of the committed Christian.

A virtuous orientation values people for more than their usefulness. Individual achievement is not pursued at the expense of justice or of community. If a fellow employee is worried or unhappy, it should be noticed and addressed with love. To seek others' approval by a hard-driving work ethic is not in the holiness deck of cards. Self-discipline is manifest by not being gossips, snoops, rumor mongers, or blamers. Reaching out is more effective than lashing out. Unbecoming behavior not only reflects poorly on an individual Catholic, but also on the Catholic Church. Catholics are not "up here" ministering to people "down there." To be cynical with a "can't do anything about it" attitude can turn people away. Courage helps identify issues that can lead to deeper connections with others. There are massive problems in society. It is not the Christian way to throw up one's hands and say nothing can be done. One does not retreat from a problem, but rather defines it, and attempts to alleviate it. Every little bit helps. To demonstrate genuine compassion and competence at the workplace is to raise up society. Therefore, honest praise is worth more than criticism. Giving praise to those who are on time, who meet deadlines, who are faithful to little things or have other good work habits should be a priority. Holding one's tongue when one feels like snapping, or being verbally abusive, is beneficial in any environment. A disagreement pleasantly expressed is an art form.

> Keep us O God, from pettiness;
> let us be large in thought, in word, in deed.
> Let us be done with faultfinding, and leave off self seeking.
> May we put away all pretense,
> and meet each other face to face—
> Without self pity and without prejudice.
> May we never be hasty in judgment and always generous.
> Let us take time for all things: Make us to grow calm, serene, gentle.

Teach us to put into action our better impulses,
straightforward and unafraid.
Grant that we may realize it is the little things that create differences;
that in the big things of life we are at one.
And may we strive to touch and to know
the great, common human heart of us all.
And, O Lord God, let us forget not to be kind.

~Mary Stuart

The Strength of Integrity

Christian integrity helps to avoid being influenced by consumer trends. Christians trust in Jesus and want to guide others to him. This happens mainly by the quality of our presence. If people are not drawn to us, they will not be drawn to Christianity. We must be Christians with integrity. Christian integrity is a wholeness of character that includes sound adherence to moral and spiritual values, freedom from deception and duplicity, and faithfulness to one's word, responsibilities and duties. To use the words of Bessie Anderson Stanley, integrity is a man (or woman) "who has lived well, laughed often and loved much; Who has gained the respect of intelligent people and the love of children. Who has filled his niche and accomplished his task; Who leaves the world better than he found it whether by a perfect poem or a rescued soul; Who never lacked appreciation of earth's beauty or failed to express it; who looked for the best in others and gave the best he had."

How do we live Christian integrity? How do we conduct ourselves, respond to others, and interpret our problems and circumstances? Indeed, every choice we make has a rating on a continuum from destructive to edifying. We strive to make choices that stimulate a virtuous cycle. To respect and appreciate all things, and to treasure love and life, to be faithful to daily spiritual practices and to work, are beautiful signs of integrity.

Trustworthiness defines a person of integrity. When helping others, many things need to remain private and personal. Prudence is the guidepost regarding when and to whom we disclose information. Every person has aspects in his or her life that should not be addressed casually. To share too much about ourselves or to be too curious about others, or about things that do not pertain to us, indicates indiscretion. Trustworthy behavior is guided by restraint and minding our own business. To say what we want when we want is not an option because it is inconsiderate and makes life difficult. When we do make poor choices, they do not dishearten us, they initiate a resolve to improve and try again. Trust helps us to have confidence in ourselves by believing in our instincts, intuition, education, experience, judgment and learning from our mistakes.

"In you O Lord, I place all my trust" (Ps 143:8). This is a lofty statement. How can we place our concerns and ourselves in the hands of God? We trust in God and we do our part. We take responsibility, but keep the way open for God's inspiration and assistance. God will help us with our responsibilities if we do what we can according to our abilities. He is with us when we sense peace and calm instead of worry and doubt. We give our major or minor needs, disappointments and irritations to him and somehow he helps us work things out. Jane Frances de Chantal tells us: "With the confidence of a son, rest in the care and love that Divine Providence has for you in all your needs. Look upon Providence as a child does its mother who loves him tenderly. You can be sure that God loves you incomparably more."

A person who practices the art of trusting in God has a better chance of practicing the art of living a regular and committed life. Because of these two qualities, a person has a mind that is less distracted and agitated and more focused and serene. Thomas Aquinas had this to say: "Be assured that he who will always walk faithfully in God's presence, always ready to give human account of all his actions, will never be separated from him by consenting to sin." To make choices concerning how to act, we consider them in the light of being a trustworthy seeker of God and helper of others. To trust in God involves letting go, taking good risks, making decisions that require the most courage, leaping into the unknown and being at ease with the consequences.

To trust is not easy these days. A few words about trusting people: Be cautious. Teresa of Avila tells us: "Consider seriously how quickly people change, and how little trust is to be had in them, and hold fast to God, who does not change." Blind trust is not always prudent. We should not trust everybody and we cannot trust nobody. If we trust everyone without reserve we will be deceived. If we cannot trust anyone we will be tormented. When our trust in another has been tarnished, it is hard to restore its original shine. We cannot trust what society says is acceptable. Even though we should be as innocent as doves, we must also be as shrewd as serpents so that we will not be deceived or used. Goethe gives us some sound, overall advice: "Treat people as if they were what they ought to be and you help them to become what they are capable of being." To trust others is to let them make their own age related decisions and hope they will learn from their mistakes.

The heart of truth is honesty. A person is as good as his or her promise. There should be no gap between what a person says and what he does. Thomas Jefferson wrote: "Honesty is the first chapter in the book of wisdom." We respect the facts even if they are unpleasant, see others as they are instead of how we want them to be and discern if what we are doing helps or hinders others. Honesty with ourselves is the biggest challenge of all. If we live up to this challenge, we need not be concerned about being clever, witty or insightful. We are genuine by just being the best we can be. Honesty can be simply summarized by living the Ten Commandments. Honesty also prompts us to speak up when someone is being treated poorly or unfairly. Even when no one is looking, we do what is right not what is easy.

Honesty fosters a more accurate appreciation and deeper consideration for serious situations that come our way. If we live in honesty and transparency, we are open to those who need us. What does this mean? We tell our loved ones where we are, where we will be going and what we will be doing. We have no concern if someone looks at the websites we visited, looks in our files, listens to our smart phone conversations, reads our emails, or knows who is on our speed dial. Acting honestly toward everyone will bear good fruit and nurture a clear conscience. It will also increase the ability to take things in stride. Taking things as they come, without undue anxiety, is an exceptional grace.

Trouble in the Workplace

Very often situations can become awkward in the workplace because of tensions between different beliefs and behaviors. Workplaces can bring on anxiety and unhappiness through egotism, competitiveness and politics that arise from fear and the human condition.

"We shall steer safely through every storm, as long as our heart is right, our intention fervent, our courage steadfast, and our trust fixed on God," wrote Frances de Sales. In spite of innumerable problems and overwhelming difficulties, we push ahead because God is with us. Making decisions within the context of our Christian teachings can be a challenge. Our call to follow Christ can leave us feeling alone, misunderstood and in pain. In our society, moral integrity and strength of soul are lonely roads on which to tread. To remain faithful to gospel ideals is to experience fragments of crucifixion. To avoid duplicity, we need to uphold the same values in our private lives as in our public lives. Instead of taking the easy way out by going with whatever is popular, we stand up for our principles. Our workplace is our challenge. Yet, even in confusing times, holiness attracts. A coworker with a problem will more likely confide in a Christian with strong family values. A chaste young single woman who regularly volunteers at a local food bank has more time to give to the needy because her life is disciplined and grounded. We strive toward a noble call. In *The Making of a Christian Leader*, Ted Engstrom wrote:

> The world needs men who cannot be bought; whose word is their bond; who put character above wealth; who possess opinions and a will; who are larger than their vocations; who do not hesitate to take chances; who will not lose their individuality in a crowd; who will be as honest in small things as in great things; who will make no compromise with wrong; whose ambitions are not confined to their own selfish desires; who will not say they do it "because everybody else does it"; who are true to their friends through good report and evil report, in adversity as well as in prosperity; who do not believe that shrewdness, cunning and hardheadedness are the best qualities for winning success; who are not ashamed or afraid to stand for the truth when it is unpopular; who say "no" with emphasis, although the rest of the world says "yes."

Holiness inspires others to do good. Staying alert is basic to a stable Christian life. Each act and each day are sufficient unto themselves. If a young woman examines her motivations, then prioritizes her tasks, she completes each activity in its turn. It is possible to be calm and unhurried and do things promptly with full attention and determination. The gentleman saint, Francis de Sales, offers these words of wisdom: "Rivers that flow gently through the plains carry along larger boats. Rains that fall gently on open fields make them fruitful in grass and grain. Torrents and rivers that spread over the land in great floods ruin the bordering country and are useless for commerce, just as in like manner heavy tempestuous rains ruin the fields and meadows. A job done too hurriedly is never well done."

When we understand that life is a journey toward union with Jesus, we are able to put our goals and milestones in proper perspective. We try to free ourselves from repeated self centered behaviors that easily enslave us. It is easy to become wrapped up in our own little world. We must define our illusions, duplicities and compulsions and confront them. This is a spiritual challenge. Character is not defined by what others think of us, but by what God knows of us. Christian living is the motivator for thinking, seriously and repeatedly, about how an individual reflects Jesus' love in conduct and lifestyle. Adverse trends in society corrupt energy, blur vision and demean humanity. For example, provocative dress is an invitation to be used as an object of pleasure alone. Crude language diminishes the dignity of the human race. Christianity affects our demeanor wherever we are. When we dress and talk like committed Christians, we act more like committed Christians. If we keep Jesus in mind we avoid rough language, demeaning jokes and negative attitudes. We dress with dignity, act with courtesy, live the virtues and quietly help those in need. These traits safeguard our souls and sanctify society. Our views, attitudes, ideas, recreational tastes, reading and entertainment, the level of luxury in which we live, our emphasis on success, power and social prestige, and how we treat others verify how we live Jesus' love. Our choice of lifestyle can illuminate or dim our Christianity. If our holiness alert system is not on, negative people can lead us into their darkness.

A Positive Outlook

When Mother Teresa returned from a trip, we always wanted to know, not only everything that she had done and accomplished, but also, naturally, what difficulties she had run into and any mean things or nasty tricks that the high ranking politicians or officials she had met had done. In short, we wanted to hear the spicy stories too.

But, Mother Teresa, as a matter of principle, never said a negative word about anyone. In response to our eager questions about whether she had been betrayed here or there, whether they had hoodwinked, manipulated or mistreated her, she usually replied, "They were so good to us!" Instead of the hoped for spicy stories, she told us how her hosts, or the government in the countries where she had been traveling, had helped with this and that, the efforts that they had made, and the successes that had resulted.

Never was there a negative word, so that once someone said, "But, Mother Teresa, surely not everything went well." Her answer came without hesitation: "You know, Father: rather excuse than accuse." I remember hearing her say this several times. On another occasion—in Moscow, after experiences with the Soviet authorities that were certainly not always pleasant—we pressed her again, but even then we got no derogatory remarks, only a lesson: "If you judge someone, then you have no time to love him."

An Indian family who had helped her a lot at the beginning of her work in the slums of Calcutta had a very special place in their hearts for Mother Teresa, so she used to go back regularly to visit that family. It is reported that on one of those visits the daughter, now an adult, was also present and she suddenly began to complain to Mother Teresa about the corruption in the Calcutta administration. You needed a bribe for everything; you couldn't get anything done without greasing palms. She wanted Mother Teresa, who had a very good reputation with the Calcutta administration, to put in a good word for a friend of hers. The young woman said, "Mother Teresa, can't you help us? Calcutta is so corrupt. You get nothing unless you bribe people."

Mother Teresa reacted as she usually did when people "were speaking darkness," as she put it, or when someone "was spreading darkness"; "Yes, they're wonderful people. They have given us so much support for our children."

The young woman would not be content with that and retorted, "Mother Teresa, the great majority of people in Calcutta are just running after money."

For the second time, Mother Teresa tried to introduce a hopeful note, and she spoke about the Hindu custom of always putting a handful of rice at the door for the poor.

The young woman was exasperated: "Mother Teresa when will you wake up? Calcutta is a hell of corruption."

There were a few seconds of painful silence. Mother Teresa remained quite calm, looked the young woman right in the eyes and said. "I know very well that there is corruption in Calcutta, but I also know that there is good, and I have decided to see the good."[3]

Jesus Christ is the source of authentic goodness and love. He loves us and counts on us to bring his love to others. As the Apostle Paul said, it is in him that we live and move and have our being. The quiet, unexcitable young woman, Gemma Galgani, remarked, "Ah, if everyone were to know how beautiful Jesus is, how amiable he is, they would all die from love."

---

3. Maasburg, *Mother Teresa of Calcutta*, 90–92.

Joseph the Worker

Joseph was the beloved husband of Mary and the beloved foster father of Jesus. The gospels describe Joseph as a *tekton*. Traditionally, the word has been translated to mean "carpenter," although the Greek term suggests an artisan with wood in general, or an artisan in iron or stone. He is honored as the epitome of the dignity of workers and the guardian of the worker's family. He was always honest, conscientious, fair and dependable. Joseph was an exemplary worker because he saw the process of working just as important as the result. All his work was done for his love of Jesus and Mary, which gave it the highest value. Joseph teaches us that our work will be as great as our intentions are pure. This includes all the small tasks we normally consider insignificant.

> Dear St. Joseph, example for all who are engaged in toil, please pray with me so that I may work in the spirit of atonement for my sins; that I may work conscientiously, keeping devotion to duty before my personal feelings; that I may work with thankfulness and joy, holding it an honor to use and develop by my labor, the gifts I have received from almighty God.
>
> Pray with me that I may work with order, peace, moderation and patience—and never shirk duty because of weariness or because of difficulties encountered; that I do my best, whether the task is easy or difficult, pleasant or unpleasant; that I keep a good sense of humor. Before all else, may I work with a right intention and with detachment from self, keeping in mind the hour of my death and the account I must give to God for misused time, for neglected talents, for good not done, and for any foolish pride in my success.
>
> All for Jesus, all through Mary, all in imitation of you, Joseph, most faithful. Amen.[4]

---

4. Adapted from a prayer by Puis X.

Suffering: Grace Unexpected

A YOUNG, SUCCESSFUL EXECUTIVE was traveling down a neighborhood street, going a bit too fast in his new Jaguar. He was watching for kids darting out from between parked cars and slowed down when he thought he saw something. As his car passed, no children appeared, but instead a large rock smashed into the Jag's side door. He slammed on the brakes and backed up to the spot where the rock had been thrown. The angry driver jumped out of the car, grabbed the nearest kid and pushed him up against a parked car. He shouted, "Who are you and what was that all about? That is a new car and the rock you threw is going to cost me a lot of money. Why did you do it?" The young boy apologized. "Please, mister, I'm sorry, but I didn't know what else to do. I threw the rock because no one would stop." With tears in his eyes, the youth pointed to a spot just around a parked car. "It's my brother. He rolled off the curb and fell out of his wheelchair and I can't lift him up." The boy asked the stunned executive, "Would you please help me get him back into his wheelchair? He's hurt and he is too heavy for me." Moved beyond words, the driver lifted the handicapped boy back into the wheelchair, took out a linen handkerchief and dabbed at the fresh scrapes and cuts. A good look told him everything was okay. "Thank you and may God bless you," the grateful child told the stranger. Too shaken up for words, the man simply watched the boy push his brother down the sidewalk. Although the damage to the Jaguar was noticeable, the driver never bothered to repair it. The dent reminded him not to go through life so fast that someone has to throw a rock at him to get his attention.

When an individual is hit with the rock of suffering, things change. There well may be lasting dents from that rock in one's life. Pain comes in many forms and on many levels. There is no escape from it. Society cannot see the value of pain and seeks to quickly alleviate it. It is true that pain can conquer, victimize or break us. It is also true that we can be stoic by placing ourselves above the pain or be a product of our pain by making it the center of our existence. However, these are not Christian options.

Pain raises questions: Is there a need to change particular areas in my lifestyle? How does the pain affect my identity? How do I deny pain? How does my suffering affect my trust in God? Serious illness can bring many changes. Independence decreases, pain increases, daily patterns change, or plans and dreams diminish or are no longer viable. To all of these adjustments there are choices to be made.

Even though we do not desire suffering, it comes to us all and when it comes, we must choose what to do with it. Responses can range from deep self-pity to creative new growth. Suffering can break us down or break us open. It can shrivel our souls or stretch them to great sanctity. God's grace helps Christians transform suffering from something that can crush into something that can sanctify.

To be one with Jesus is to place our sufferings in his hands. He, in turn, will place them in the hands of God the Father, who will send the Holy Spirit to strengthen us. Thus, suffering can bind us to the Triune God and be an effective act of love. Jesus did not bring suffering into the world. We did. Jesus did not promote suffering; he sanctified it through his passion and death. Jesus made suffering inseparable from his redeeming love.

Because of Christ's redeeming love, personal suffering is never useless. It is a most effective gift to give to God for the good of our fellow human beings. Jesus helps humankind to bear pain and grow with it. He is all mercy and love and the source for the greatest consolation. If we harness the positive elements of pain, we can resist being helplessly swept away by it. Pain can bring humanity closer to Jesus. Indeed, if there were no pain and suffering there would be no healing and joy. Henry Ward Beecher wrote: "Affliction comes to us all, not to make us sad, but sober; not to make us sorry, but wise; not to make us despondent, but by its darkness to refresh us, as the night refreshes the day; not to impoverish, but to enrich us, as the plough enriches the field; to multiply our joy, as the seed by planting is multiplied a thousand-fold."

Many people who are marginalized by illness are peaceful and serene because they believe they work together with Jesus in the redemption of humanity. Today, Jesus suffers in his mystical body. When Christians offer their pain to Jesus, they share his suffering for the salvation of souls. The life of a chronically ill person in a hospital bed is far from worthless. The tragedy of suffering is useless suffering. When we recognize the transcendent purpose behind suffering, it loses its sting and advances the salvation of humanity. When pain that seems too much to bear is endured for Jesus' sake, it lifts one's heart to know that this causes grace to work somewhere. Painful and sinful humanity unites with the goodness and mercy of God. Within the mystical body of Christ, those who suffer help to save souls.

The Cross

Companionship with Jesus as a healer, teacher or shepherd is comforting. However, there is no natural inclination to companion with the suffering Jesus. At the foot of the cross, grace reveals that Christians are broken and in need of repair. When anyone is confused, frustrated or helpless, it is difficult to see things as Jesus would see them. How desperately we need him! The cross wakes Christians up from spiritual lethargy. The more a person looks at Jesus crucified, the more she sees his strength. Prayer at the foot of the cross can make Christians more thoughtful, more sensitive and can uncover inner courage previously unknown. In suffering there is a call to divine intimacy not found in other circumstances.

The cross is a part of every good life and every good work. With the aid of grace, crosses give a person more authenticity and depth. The cross can take a Christian from knowing about Jesus to completely trusting in him. We cannot walk the road of holiness without passing through deserts of suffering. These desert treks are dry, empty and seemingly trackless with unseen prickly cactuses that stab us when we least expect it. Walter Ciszek, SJ, in his book *He Leadeth Me*, wrote:

> There are moments of crisis in every life, moments of anxiety and fear; moments of frustration and opposition, moments sometimes even of terror. The kingdom of Christ—that kingdom of justice and peace, of love and of truth—has not yet been achieved here on earth; it has begun, but much remains to be done before it can reach its fullness and all creation will have again been made new according to the mind of the Father. Evil still exists alongside justice like the cockle among the wheat, hatred alongside love, the good with the bad, the sinner along with the saint. None of us, then, can escape the tensions of this imperfect world.[1]

1. Ciszek, *He Leadeth Me*, 186. Walter Ciszek was a Polish-American Jesuit priest who conducted clandestine missionary work in the Soviet Union between 1939 and 1963. He was imprisoned and spent twenty-three years in Soviet prisons and the labor camps of Siberia, before being allowed to return to the United States. When he could, he

When life seems unbearable, we look at Jesus. He was perfect and blameless, yet seized, spit upon, scourged, crowned with thorns and nailed to a cross. When we ask why, the word to remember is love, Jesus' great love, for us.

Therefore, it is a very good habit to unite our suffering with Jesus crucified. This unexplainable union transforms suffering and increases the sanctification of the faithful. Evil was mastered by good and hate overcome by love when Jesus died. The mystery of redemptive suffering is not for us to understand, because we cannot. It is for us to live.

When tragedy or horror comes our way, we find solace and comfort in uniting that which we do not understand with the crucifixion of Christ. Redemptive suffering is a gift beloved by God. The giver prays for a stout heart. Surrendering difficulties in the dark shadow of Good Friday is only possible because one sees light on the horizon of Easter Sunday. In time and with grace, through the mystery of Christ's love, there is tranquility. Resurrection is coming. On the cross, Jesus drowned all sin in the infinite ocean of his mercy and his mercy endures forever. The mystery of the cross shows that pain is never isolated or separated from love. Ongoing suffering draws a person deeper into the mystery of God.

Toward the Good

A desert mother wrote: "A great deal is gained spiritually by bearing illness quietly and giving thanks to God." Pain must be respected. If we try to see it as a teacher, we can work with it, or around it, constructively. When pain tests us, our response is personal. It reflects the character of our faith. It can bring out the best or the worst in us. A simple cold can be a minor inconvenience or a major disaster. Our hardship can make us and those around us miserable or it can be an example of faithful endurance.

Each one of us is flawed in some way, but we cannot let our flaws control us. If our focus on negative attributes is excessive, it drains energy that can be used for a better purpose. If we redirect our energy to focus on positive attributes, pain can transform us. Camu wrote: "One ounce of patient suffering is worth far more than a pound of action."

---

cared for the spiritual needs of the prisoners with whom he lived, providing Mass and the sacraments. Father Ciszek wrote of his experiences in two books, *With God in Russia* and *He Leadeth Me*. He died in New York on December 8, 1984.

Suffering: Grace Unexpected

A degenerative illness may prevent us from doing things that we once enjoyed. However, perhaps these things kept us absorbed in ourselves or used time that should have been spent on our responsibilities. Chronic ill health can be a channel for holiness. Somehow, we meet God in our pain. We are reminded by the convert and author Leon Bloy: "Man has places in his heart which do not yet exist, and into them enters suffering, that they might have existence." We should not stop trying to understand and appreciate the mystery of suffering. It is a great opportunity to transform negative thinking about limitations into positive energy about potential. Every person has talents, unencumbered by suffering, which, when used in union with Jesus, further the good of the Church and the world.

When an individual is very ill, a good place to imagine oneself is standing beside Mary at the foot of the cross. At this most difficult moment in her life, she accepted the mantle of universal motherhood and became the source of our strength in life's darkest hours. Bernadette saw Mary at Lourdes. Bernadette offers more suggestions on how to cope with suffering. During her long nights of pain, she used to say the rosary. At other times, she imagined herself in adoration before the tabernacle. Pinned to her bed curtains was a picture of a monstrance. "I am happy in my sleepless hours uniting myself with our Lord. One glance at this picture gives me the longing and strength to immolate myself when I am feeling my loneliness and my pains," she said to Mother Audidier.

God, who is all love, is the only one who can bring true light into the dark depths of human sorrow. An individual can make a breakthrough into God's love through his own suffering. It forces him to look outside himself and embrace the possibilities that exist beyond the pain. An individual may discover new talents, such as painting with watercolors or writing poetry. If he has compassion toward himself, he should have more compassion toward others. To see one's limitations and insufficiencies without self-pity can encourage others to do likewise.

To strive to be like Jesus without drama or self aggrandizement is a sign of humility. When in pain our prayer may be a soft sigh or quiet tears. These prayers can be more profound than long prayers of supplication. Dark episodes help Christians sit still, listen to God and find the sacred in the gloom. Only when a person drinks the dregs of darkness can he savor the sparkle of light. A journey to light is a journey to deeper humility. Darkness makes light easier to see. And by this light one can see God working everywhere.

> Fierce are the waves, Lord, rough the seas,
> And dark, so dark the night.
> I beg of you to grant me, please,
> On lonely vigil, light.
>
> ~Edith Stein

Responding to creative graces that come from suffering alters our outlook toward negative events and circumstances. With God's help, even the worst of events can lead to good. It is possible to emerge from a painful experience with greater character, stronger virtues and deeper wisdom. Feeling good pales in comparison to knowing good and doing good. How Christians help others with their pain shows how Christ is manifest in the world today. Thomas à Kempis urges Christians forward: "He who knows how to suffer will enjoy much peace. Such a one is a conqueror of himself and lord of the world, a friend of Christ and a heir of heaven."

Margaret

Margaret of Castello was born in 1287 to a noble family in the castle of Metola, southeast of Florence, Italy. She was a dwarf, blind, and hunchbacked, with a malformed short right leg. Her rich parents kept her out of sight because they were ashamed of her. The maid, who named the child Margaret, cared for her within the castle until she was six. Then her parents moved her to a cell attached to a forest church where she stayed for fourteen years. It was through the family chaplain that Margaret came to know God and received the sacraments. When she was twenty, her parents, seeking a miracle, took her to the tomb of a holy Franciscan named Fra Giacomo, enshrined in the Franciscan church in the village of Citta di Castello. When no miracle occurred, they abandoned her. Margaret's faith and courage inspired a group of poor women to help her survive. Later, she entered a cloistered convent. However, her sincere faith and dedication to an austere lifestyle caused the nuns, who were used to a comfortable lifestyle, to send her away. Taken in by a villager, Margaret became a member of what is now called the Lay Dominicans of Castello, where she lived an exemplary life of prayer, penance, and charity. Despite her handicaps, Margaret was serene, cheerful, and courageous. She never complained or lost heart. She did not know discouragement. She found strength in prayer, daily Mass, and Holy Communion. Jesus, Mary, Joseph, and Saint Dominic were her guides. Margaret looked at suffering with the eyes of faith. She did not know why God permitted her to have so many afflictions. She did know that he was an infinitely loving and kind Father, who never permitted a single misfortune without good reason. Margaret wondered why people pitied her because she saw it as a privilege to suffer with Christ. Suffering was her way to heaven. Pain made Margaret empathetic and understanding toward others. She visited prisoners, cared for the sick, and comforted the dying. Reports circulated that miracles sometimes followed Margaret's prayers. Margaret did not allow her disabilities to lead her to self-pity or bitterness. Instead, she focused on the love of God and brought that love to those around her. When Margaret died in 1320, a great crowd that gathered for her funeral demanded that she be buried inside the church, but the priest refused. When a girl disabled by an accident was miraculously cured during the funeral, the priest relented. Since her death at age thirty-three, she has continued to help those who pray to her. Many cures have been attributed to her intercession. Margaret of Castello was declared blessed on October 19, 1609. She helps those who are unwanted and abandoned and inspires those who are discouraged and tempted to self-pity. Her feast day is April 13th. She is a patron of the pro-life movement and of those with disabilities.

Great Love

Holiness is a universal call for all. We go to God together. Christians who accept suffering can be an inspiration to others. Christ teaches his followers how to use pain wisely. To surrender that which troubles us, in union with Christ to the Father, is an exquisite expression of love. Every expression of this love mitigates the world's sorrows. Consequently, personal suffering is never worthless. It is a gift to be given to God so people can become more aware of, and open to, his love.

Healing takes time. Patience fosters perseverance and perseverance deepens hope. Through suffering, God's love pours into our hearts in ways we do not understand. When someone is open to the light of God, healing begins, not only for the person, but also through him or her for the whole world. Despite the difficulties and disappointments in life, a certain harmony is maintained because everything is in the hands of God. Jesus changes emptiness into fullness in unimagined ways. Those who walk close to the Lord bear great trials and burn with great love. Love is present in humanity in unexpected corridors that must be passed through in life.

An individual who sat in an emergency waiting room noticed a man in a wheelchair in considerable pain. His wife was by his side. For a half hour, the couple never exchanged a word; they just held hands, looking intently at each other. Once or twice the woman patted the man's face. The person who watched this said the feeling of love was so tangible in the room that she felt she was sharing their silent communion. Their silent love was joyful and portrayed the fullness of a human relationship. Spiritual silence is like that. Love does not necessarily require words, but it often thrives in silence.

The Garden

Each person's boat of life travels through shadows of suffering and sunbeams of love. How an individual interprets and responds to suffering and love is an important part of his or her expression of being a unique Christian. John of the Cross once wrote: "And I saw the river over which every soul must pass to reach the kingdom of heaven, and the name of the river was suffering. And I saw the boat which carries souls across the river, and the name of the boat was love."

Pain is subjective. When offered with love it is also sacrificial. Sacrificial love is evident everyday. A bone tired mother tends to her sick child in the middle of the night. A father works at a monotonous job for the good of his family. A single adult takes care of her infirm parents. A nurse tends to critically ill patients. A grandmother cares for her orphaned grandson who has terminal cancer.

> Down shadowy lanes, across strange streams
> Bridged over by our broken dreams;
> Behind the misty caps of years,
> Beyond the great salt fount of tears,
> The garden lies. Strive as you may,
> You cannot miss it in your way.
> All paths that have been or shall be,
> Pass somewhere through Gethsemane.

Suffering: Grace Unexpected

> All those who journey, soon or late,
> Must pass within the garden's gate;
> Must kneel alone in darkness there,
> And battle with some fierce despair.
> God pity those who cannot say,
> "Not mine but thine," who only pray,
> "Let this cup pass," and cannot see
> The purpose in Gethsemane.
>
> ~Ella Wheeler Wilcox

Anne Morrow Lindbergh, and her husband Charles, faced an unimaginable horror when their infant son was kidnapped and murdered. In her book *Hour of Gold, Hour of Lead*, she wrote: "The long road of insight, suffering, healing and rebirth is best illustrated in the Christian religion by the suffering, death and resurrection of Christ."

Jesus never said our lives would be smooth sailing. He did say, "I am with you." We join ourselves to Christ and bondage is changed to bonding. In subtle and quiet ways, Jesus works within our troubles to transform us and infuse our souls with peace. Personal disasters yield hidden blessings that console and inspire in the midst of problems. What appears to be a tragedy can often turn out to have hidden blessings that surprise us. For instance, A husband takes a leave of absence from work to nurse his sick wife and discovers an intimacy they have never known before.

When suffering takes its toll, a person can imagine a grapevine and the pruning process. When grapevines are trimmed by a gifted hand, the quantity of fruit they yield decreases, but the remaining grapes improve in quality and produce finer wine. The wine is sharper in color, richer in aroma and deeper in taste. If the vine was not pruned, and all the grapes used, the wine would be watery in color, weak in aroma and have no distinct flavor. Restricting the vine allowed it to channel all its resources into the remaining grapes, heightening the quality of their yield. In a similar manner, an individual is pruned by suffering. It limits him, but enriches his tree of life. He may no longer be able to do certain activities, but finds new activities that could be more enriching. Chronic disease or disability can give him a broader and deeper perspective of life. Disease and suffering are not an automatic channel to holiness. A person chooses his disposition. Cardinal Suenens once said, "We must raise our eyes to Calvary, if we are to grasp the import of redemptive suffering." As Christians, we live in the shadow of the cross, but must watch for the light of resurrection.

Joy comes out of sorrow when we surrender to God in our pain. Hope believes Jesus steps into the storms of life and calms the raging waters that threaten to drown us. Only by keeping our gaze on Jesus can we move through the storm toward the light. We endure the worst because we believe the promises of God. To remain steadfast demands a lot of determination. John Cassian is very direct: "To cling always to God and to the things of God, this must be our major effort, this must be the road that the heart follows unswervingly."

"O Marguerite, my sister, while I, dedicated to the positive forces of the universe was wandering over the continents and seas passionately watching all the hues of the earth arise, you, motionless and prostrate, were silently transforming, at the very depths of your being, the darkest shadows into Light. Tell me, in the Eyes of the Creator, which of us two will have played the better role?"[2]

Healing Ways

A person can be healed even if he is not cured. Healing takes place at a deeper level than a cure. This is spiritual healing. Teresa of Avila advises: "The greatest honor God can grant to a soul is not to give much to it but to ask much from it." If an individual is able to look into the face of her pain and see the face of Jesus, then she embraces her suffering as a true Christian. Faith and prayer do not remove hard times from a person's life. They help a person through them.

Perhaps God made Christians fragile so that they would be more caring toward each other. Christians are precious to God and need each other. Weakness or disability can connect people to one another. Christians weave the threads of life together more strongly when they support each other. An expressed need may begin a serious conversation or friendship. A small request may help another feel wanted. Although an immensely popular image today, rugged independence disconnects people from each other and

---

2. Teilhard de Chardin, *Activation of Energy*, 249. Pierre Teilhard de Chardin (1881–1955) was a Jesuit priest and paleontologist who worked to understand faith and evolution. His life included priesthood, living and working in the front lines of war, field work, exploring the early origins of the human race, and adventurous travels of discovery in the backlands of China. He led a vibrant intellectual life through the development of his imaginative, mystical writings on the evolutionary nature of the world and the cosmos.

weakens family, church and community. Interdependence, rooted in gospel values, bonds people together. Problems shared become lighter loads. Sharing wisdom that comes from personal wounds helps people to know each other better. Sharing different solutions to problems facilitates moving forward. Yes, grace often has unpleasant wrappings, but when the wrappings are removed a person may find precious pearls.

After he was diagnosed with a serious disease, John Paul II said: "I too know, through personal experience, the suffering that physical disability brings, the weakness brought on by illness, the lack of energy for work and the sense of being unable to lead a normal life. But I also know, and I would like to make clear to you, that this suffering also has another, sublime aspect. Namely, it gives a great spiritual capacity, for suffering is a purification for the one who suffers and for others, and if it is lived in the Christian dimension, it can be transformed into a gift offered to complete in one's own flesh that which is lacking in the sufferings of Christ for his body which is the Church."

An orientation toward the positive aspects of suffering helps humankind become more effective in caring for others. To extend a loving Christian presence by listening is an authentic sign of care. Listening is a prerequisite to action. To be in the dark with someone who is in the dark creates a bond. Sharing darkness takes more courage than standing outside the dark and talking about the light. Sharing someone's pain by listening with the heart can provide more solace and be a greater help than giving advice or explaining strategies. A quiet, open availability, with time to wonder, a hand to hold, and a shoulder to cry on, seems so little but can be so much.

A couple who lost their teenage son, killed in a drive-by shooting several years ago, spends quiet time with parents experiencing a similar bereavement at the funeral home. Their silent presence says more than most sympathetic words offered by well-meaning people. Silent presence can be the first step on the long road of healing.

"To suffer and be happy although suffering, to have one's feet on the earth, to walk on the dirty and rough paths of this earth and yet to be enthroned with Christ at the Father's right hand, to laugh and cry with the children of this world and ceaselessly sing the praises of God with the choirs of angels—this is the life of the Christian until the morning of eternity breaks forth."[3]

3. Stein, *Hidden Life*, 92.

Everyday Holiness

Lest We Forget

The sounds of the last departing convoy had long since died away. The scene was oppressive, as was the sudden emptiness of the vast stores which had so recently been brimful of treasure.

In a corner, spread eagle on the floor and covered with dust and snow, lay a Teddy bear, ignored in the haste of the convoy's departure. An old Teddy bear he appeared to be, with one leg missing, his fur torn and mildewed, straw trailing from his burst seams and his squeak long ago reduced to silence. For four years he had lain at the bottom of a huge pile of toys, thousands and thousands of toys from all over Europe. For these were no ordinary stores. This was Auschwitz, evil smelling and pestilential. The year was 1944.

Mis (pronounced Mish) was not really so very old at all, although it seemed to him that more than a hundred years had passed since his world had come to an end. Before that, he had been a proud and happy bear; he had known a white house, and sunlight, picnics on the grass, the laughter of children, the joy of sleeping in cool white sheets with Stani.

Stani . . . Mis felt the need for tears when he thought of his young master, the little boy with the tousled head and wide grin, who had whispered secrets to him in the dark, and had hugged him tight, calling him "darling bear," and vowing never to be parted from him. It had been Stani's fourth birthday, he remembered, when the soldiers came. The honey cake had been left uneaten and the presents were still in their gay wrappings, for there had been no time to open them. Stani, not understanding, had run for his bear and held him close as the family had been herded into the street. With hundreds of others, they had been marched to the station. Mis had thought it was a game at first, though Stani had held him clutched close to his heart. But at the station it was a game no longer. They had been forced into trucks as though they were cattle, and hell had begun. No air, no water, no light, no hope. He could still hear the cries of the children, the despairing curses of the men. A few had died there, others had gone mad. How could one ever forget the appalling fetid stench, and the fear, the terrible fear?

How long the journey had lasted Mis did not know, it seemed to be several weeks because this had become but a part of the greater nightmare. He didn't know whether it was night or day when they arrived at the station and, bewildered and terrified, were lined up on a ramp alongside. He remembered the doll a soldier had snatched from a child and stamped on the ground. Then had come the parting. Stani's father had been dragged away with the other men, and Stani and his mother, clinging together, had been stripped of their possessions. How Stani had screamed and fought to keep him, but it was no use, even though Mis had lost a leg in the struggle. He had watched and had heard the hiss of escaping gas, the agonizing cries, and even though he had waited and waited in conditions too terrible to describe, he had never seen either of them again. Now, having heard the curses and awful talk of the guards, he knew that the only way out of Auschwitz was through the furnaces whose chimneys smoked day and night.

Mis now found himself in the store house in an indescribable scene. There were thousands of toys, dragged like himself from their sorrowing owners; but there were stranger things besides . . . piles of clothes, shoes, spectacles, human hair, photograph albums, even gold teeth and artificial limbs.

Was it really only four short years ago? The soldiers had cleared most of the store houses now, and sent their loot to Germany. With their going, Mis sensed obscurely that the long night was passing, but he felt too tired and too old to care. Thoughts and memories so crowded in on him that he only gradually became aware of a new sensation. Smoke was filling the store and tongues of flame were already licking greedily at the walls. Mis's eyes were stinging, and as the swirling fire roared nearer, the past and present became a confused blur in his mind. This was how it had to end: he felt almost happy now. As the flames scorched his fur, his last thoughts were with Stani, the cool sheets and the white house, a world ago when life had been sweet.

Epilogue: Some of Mis's companions who survived today lie in huge piles in glass cases together with babies' bottles, booties and dolls. They are there as a part of the museum at Auschwitz for those people who never suffered in the concentration camps to come and see. The world forgets that Stani was only one of twenty million who died in Auschwitz and other camps.[4]

The atrocities of World War II are beyond description. Yet, within those atrocities, there were people who positively responded to God's grace and became beacons of hope to those around them. The love of Christ impelled them to embrace the cross with love in their hearts. Edith Stein was Jewish. She was a philosopher, writer, teacher, and convert to the Catholic

---

4. Sue Ryder and Mary Craig of the Forgotten Allies Trust, quoted in Hutchings, *Teddy Bears*.

Faith. When she was forty-two, she entered a Carmelite monastery in Germany and became a nun. Along with her sister Rosa, she was killed at Auschwitz in 1942. During her week of imprisonment at Auschwitz, Edith showed remarkable interior strength that encouraged her fellow prisoners. She helped mothers feed and bathe their little children, even when the mothers had given up and were neglecting these tasks. During this war, people risked their lives to aid those who were persecuted by the Nazis. An unknown number of them offered assistance. Corrie ten Boom was a Dutch Christian, who with her father and other family members provided shelter in their home for Jewish and other refugees and helped many Jews escape the Nazi Holocaust. After the war she became an inspirational writer and speaker. Titus Brandsma, a Dutch Carmelite priest and professional journalist, said: "The one who wants to win the world for Christ must risk coming into conflict with it." He refused to silence the religious press and spoke openly against the Nazis. For this he was arrested and sent to a succession of prisons and concentration camps where he brought comfort and peace to his fellow prisoners and did good even to his tormentors. In 1942, after much suffering and humiliation, he was killed at Dachau. Jeanne Damman, a young Catholic teacher before the war, served as principal of an underground school for Jewish children in Brussels. When the school closed because it had become too dangerous for the children to attend, she joined the Jewish Defense Committee. She rescued many children.[5] A Polish Franciscan priest and publisher, Maximillian Kolbe, was sentenced to hard labor at the death camp in Auschwitz. He offered his life in exchange for that of a family man. He is remembered for his prophetic words, "Hatred is not a creative force. Only love is a creative power." Monsignor Hugh O'Flaherty had extraordinary intellectual gifts, which he used in the service of the Church and the Jewish community in Rome. His main Nazi rivals, and assassination attempts, could not stop his efforts to assist the Jews in Italy through a vast, complex underground network.

    Many of us will not be called to respond to large crosses that result from great wars, serious illnesses or major tragedies. However, none of us will escape from the small crosses that seem like unending pinpricks in daily life. Sometimes minor disappointments, small irritants, carelessness and irksome people seem to greet us at every turn. In whatever form our crosses take, we find revitalization and reassurance in the words of this old hymn.

    5. "Heroes and Heroines of the Holocaust," www.isurvived.org/TOC-II.html.

Suffering: Grace Unexpected

Take up your cross the Savior said,
If you would my disciple be;
Take up your cross with willing heart,
And humbly follow after me.

Take up your cross, let not the weight
Fill your weak spirit with alarm;
My strength shall bear your spirit up,
And brace your heart, and nerve your arm.

Take up your cross, heed not the shame,
And let your foolish heart be still;
The Lord for you accepted death
Upon a cross on Calv'ry's hill.

Take up your cross, then in his strength,
And calmly ev'ry danger brave.
It guides you to a better home
And leads to victory o'er the grave.

Take up your cross and follow Christ,
Nor think til death to lay it down;
For only those who bear the cross
May hope to wear the glorious crown.

~Charles W. Everest
(1814–1877)

Perseverance: Like a Turtle on the Trail

THERE IS A SIMPLE story that is often used to teach a profound lesson. It comes from Aesop's Fables. Once there was a rabbit who was in a race with a turtle. As he dashed away from the starting line, the rabbit thought he had an easy win. He got so far ahead of the turtle that he stopped and rested. Meanwhile the turtle just kept moving along at a steady pace. He was consistent. He maintained his regular speed from start to finish. There were no sudden bursts of speed or flashy shows of superiority. The rabbit woke from his nap and saw that the turtle was just about to cross the finish line. The rabbit took off, and ran as fast as he could. Alas, the turtle was too far ahead and there was no way the rabbit could catch up. The spectators watching the race were quite surprised to see the slow turtle cross the finish line ahead of the speedy rabbit.

A moral of the story is that the race of life is not won by the fastest runner or the one who gets the biggest lead at the start. The race is won by participants who maintain a consistent, regular pace from start to finish. A consistent routine is necessary in eating and exercise, in doctor and dentist checkups, in financial planning, in labor and leisure and in other necessities of life. Most importantly, there should be a regular practice of spiritual duties and responsibilities. Winston Churchill wrote: "Never give up! Never give in! Never, Never, Never, Never—in anything great or small, large or petty—never give in except to convictions of honor and good sense."

Father Patrick Rager lived these words of Winston Churchill. Affectionately known as Father Paddy, he loved everything Irish, and was a man of many talents. Born on August 14, 1959, in West Homestead, Pennsylvania, he attended St. Mary Magdalene School where he served as an altar boy. At Central Catholic High School in Pittsburgh, Paddy excelled in both athletics and academics. Today his picture hangs in their alumni hall of fame. In 1981, he earned a bachelor's degree from Duquesne University where he studied theology and psychology. While attending Duquesne, he earned his emergency medical technician certificate and served in the Air Force Reserves for two years achieving the rank of lieutenant. In the same year, he earned a master's degree in theology from Christ the King Seminary in New York and a master's degree in clinical psychopathology from St. Bonaventure University in New York. On May 11, 1985, he was ordained to the priesthood by Bishop Anthony Bevilacqua at St. Paul Cathedral in Pittsburgh. His first assignment was as parochial vicar at St. Sylvester in Brentwood, a Pittsburgh suburb, where he served from 1985 to 1987.

The first sign of illness appeared when he was a seminarian. His knee gave out during a baseball game. More falls and weakening lead to many medical tests and several misdiagnoses. Finally, after fifteen years, a diagnosis of ALS (amyotrophic lateral sclerosis), more commonly known as Lou Gehrig's disease, a slow and fatal paralysis, was made. Father Paddy's condition deteriorated and in 1987, he moved into an apartment in his parents' home. His priesthood changed direction there. Although he was confined to a wheelchair and eventually bedridden, he did not stop serving others. He wrote articles for Catholic publications. He developed a telephone and mail ministry that offered prayer, support, encouragement and counseling for persons with disabilities. After an article about him appeared in a national Catholic newsweekly, this ministry expanded to people in different areas of the world. Even with his many physical limitations, Father Paddy's priesthood was incredibly alive and strong. His great love for Jesus showed in Father Paddy's joyful attitude. He would flash a radiant smile and his dark eyes lit up when a joke or funny story was afoot. He enjoyed watching football games on TV, especially when his favorite team, the Pittsburgh Steelers, played. He focused on the lighter side of things, the goodness of life, and rarely complained. He was more concerned about hearing what others had to say than talking about himself. His strong devotion to Mary was revealed in his attentiveness and readiness to offer hope. He wrote: "Storms arrive in all of our lives with some regularity. Many times they arrive without warning. They test our strength and resolve. In these difficult circumstances, we must remember that Jesus is in the boat with us on this chaotic, turbulent sea of life, just as he was in the boat with the apostles, calming them as he rebuked the winds and the waters. For the moment, he may appear silent, but he never forsakes us." A priest wrote to him: "Perhaps you have been selected as a martyr witness to many of the rest of us who should be better priests." When he could no longer speak, he wrote using eye movements and a computer screen. Father Paddy's priesthood was used in a way he could not have imagined at ordination. On the 20th of July 2010, at the age of fifty, he went home to Jesus from the home where he was born and raised.

Father Paddy's former bishop, Cardinal Donald Wuerl of Washington, DC, said: "He really was an example of heroic virtue." Indeed, Father Paddy never gave up. He exemplified everyday holiness in prayer, in service and in suffering. Along with Paul the Apostle, he could write: "I rejoice in my sufferings. In my body I do all that I can to fill up what has yet to be endured by Christ for the sake of his body, the Church" (Col 1:24). Testimonies are being gathered to support a potential cause for his sainthood.

A Chinese Proverb says: The man who removed the mountain began by carrying away small stones. What at first seems impossible becomes possible with perseverance. Perseverance is necessary in any good deed or worthy work. It is a worthy practice to repeatedly ask God for perseverance in order to stay on the straight and narrow Christian path. It is so easy to slip into sin, but deep in the heart no one wants to do that. A great deed or good work has less to do with the degree of greatness or goodness, and has more to do with sticking with the deed or work. Especially after the good feelings or sweet satisfaction wears thin. Grace and persistence help Christians remain steadfast to the end in spite of discouragement, oppression, opposition or set backs.

Perseverance contradicts any quick solution or popular trend. Progress usually happens slowly. One only needs to look at the Grand Canyon. No rock is so hard that it cannot be slowly worn down by water. Three human elements are similar to that water: attention, determination and persistence. They grow like beautiful flowers on a trellis. They form a continuum of support for action in spite of hard hearted people, serious difficulties or unexpected problems.

When the house lights dimmed and the concert was about to begin, a mother had just returned to her seat and discovered her child was missing. At that moment, the curtains parted and the spotlights focused on the impressive Steinway piano at the center of the stage. The mother gasped as she saw her little boy sitting at the keyboard, innocently picking out the children's tune. "Twinkle, Twinkle Little Star." At that moment, the great piano master quietly made his entrance. He quickly moved to the piano, and whispered in the boy's ear, "Don't quit. Keep playing." Then, leaning over, the piano master reached down with his left hand and began augmenting the tune. Soon his right arm reached around to the other side of the child, and he added a running obbligato. Together, the old master and the young novice transformed what could have been a frightening situation into a wonderfully creative experience. The audience was so mesmerized that they couldn't recall what else the great master played. They only remembered "Twinkle, Twinkle Little Star." Is that the way it is with God? What is accomplished on one's own is rarely noteworthy. On long term projects a person can try his best, but the results are not always like graceful, flowing music. However, with the hand of God, a life's work can truly be beautiful. If an individual listens carefully, he can hear the voice of the Master, whispering, "Don't quit. Keep trying." God is there, like the piano master, turning one's feeble attempts into true masterpieces. Life is more accurately measured by lives touched than by things done. Let us not ignore the gentle voice in our ear, "Don't quit. Keep playing."

Lion Hearted

When things are going well it is not known how much perseverance a person has. It is tested by trials. People with determination work through problems and will not let difficulties break them. Rather, they bend and grow with them.

We are consoled by the words of Julian of Norwich: "He said not, 'Thou shalt not be tempted, thou shalt not be travailed, thou shalt not be afflicted,' but he said. 'Thou shalt not be overcome.'" It is good to keep the last phrase in mind. The turtle kept going even though he didn't hear crowds cheering him on, fans thinking he was oh so cute, or people betting that he would win the race. If he was discouraged, he was not overcome by it. He kept on plodding along. At times family, coworkers, friends, even the one dearest to our heart can rub us the wrong way or get on our nerves. However, perseverance helps bypass the feelings at the moment and concentrate on the commitments in a life.

It is fortunate that what is ahead on our road of life is unknown. If it were known how long it would take to fulfill a desire or dream, a person might stop trying. The same may be true for trials and suffering that may come along. Discouragement comes to us all and is a part of life. Comments like "a good Christian is never discouraged," "smile when you're feeling blue," or "grin and bear it," disregard human emotions that are very real and appropriate. People who habitually use these phrases may specialize in bringing sunshine cakes to those they visit, but these cakes are imitation. They come into a hospital room wreathed in smiles and full of happy chatter. What are they really saying? Don't be discouraged while I am here? I don't want to be involved in your pain or my pain? Their sunshine cakes are more like chicken sandwiches.

If we pray about discouragement and talk about it to wise people, we have taken a great step forward. When discouragement is acknowledged, expressed and identified, it becomes a stimulant for action that brings positive change. Pain behind discouragement is real; it cannot be denied or wished away. After it reveals new knowledge, discouragement can be released. When released, courage and strength are reestablished. Discouragement is not a pit in which to reside, it is a tunnel through which to pass.

> I've dreamed many dreams that never came true,
> I've seen them vanish at dawn;
> But I've realized enough of my dreams, thank God,
> To make me want to dream on.
>
> I've prayed many prayers when no answer came,
> I've waited patient and long;
> But answers have come to enough of my prayers
> To make me keep praying on.
>
> I've trusted many a friend who failed
> And left me to weep alone;
> But I've found enough of my friends true blue
> To make me keep trusting on.
>
> I've sown many seeds that fell by the way
> For the birds to feed upon;
> But I've held enough golden sheaves in my hand,
> To make me keep sowing on.
>
> I've drained the cup of disappointment and pain,
> I've gone many days without song,
> But I've sipped enough nectar from the rose of life
> To make me want to live on.
>
> ~Charles Allen

Perseverance: Like a Turtle on the Trail

The Secret of Abundant Living

Determination takes courage. It is not the reckless courage of youth. It is the mental or moral strength to persevere, to venture out, and to withstand danger and the fear of difficulties. Courageous people meet difficulty with fortitude and resilience. They bounce back from trials with stronger determination. Yes, they may fail many times, but they begin anew. The wisdom of Francis de Sales sustains us: "Be patient with everyone, but above all with yourself. I mean, do not be disturbed because of your imperfections and always rise up bravely from a fall." If we pack "determination" in our travel gear, discouragement is like spending a short time in a bad motel. As travelers, this is acknowledged when we pack up and move on.

A story about a donkey can teach us about perseverance. One day a farmer's donkey fell down a well. The animal cried piteously as the farmer tried to figure out what to do. Finally, he decided the animal was old, and the well needed to be covered up. It just wasn't worth it to pull out the donkey. The farmer invited all his neighbors to come over and help him. They all began to shovel dirt into the well. At first, the donkey realized what was happening and cried terribly. Then, to everyone's amazement, he quieted down. A few shovel loads later, the farmer finally looked down the well and was astonished at what he saw. With every shovel of dirt that hit his back the donkey would shake it off and take a step up. Pretty soon everyone was amazed as the donkey stepped up over the edge of the well and trotted off.

Life is going to shovel all kinds of dirt on us. The key to getting out of the dirt is to shake it off and take a step up. Each trouble can be a stepping stone, a reminder to keep moving and never give up. Life takes a lot of shaking off and stepping up. Trials vary in intensity and in time. They can resemble a twilight, grayness, blackness or anything in between. They can last for a day, a week, a year or perhaps many years. Perseverance helps us work through a crisis. A crisis can result from exhaustion, alienation, job loss, illness, family problems or bankruptcy. During these times, a person can see himself as helpless, powerless and dependent. The veneer of personal control disappears. However, consider the donkey who used his misfortune to rise above his plight. God's grace can guide a person to use unfortunate circumstances to develop creativity and teach others. Over time, a loss may result in a good that would not have come about without the loss.

Perseverance maintains a measured pace in life. It helps an individual see life through Jesus' eyes rather than through his own. How people spend their days reveals much about what they value in life. Often we change for the better without being aware of the change. The shifting sands of desires concerning the self are slowly replaced by the rock solid wisdom of Jesus' desires for humanity. Christian perseverance is not found in self-serving conditions or calculations, rarely complains and has no agendas, ulterior motives or other self focused traits. The ideals of Christianity can be like a river that flows from the consumeristic, driven rapids of the present to the hopeful placid streams of what will be in eternity; from the fragmented alienation of current situations to the unity and peace of God's promises. Perseverance in seeking less for personal benefit and more for others' welfare keeps the river flowing to the celestial sea. Hugh Feiss counsels us: "Make do with sufficiency rather than abundance or luxury. If this means owning one less car, using the library more, eating simpler, less expensive food and eating at home rather than in restaurants, making fewer trips to the theater, it is perhaps a blessing in disguise. At least necessity and social obligations—to conserve resources, avoid pollution, strengthen the family—will often coincide."

The mind can resemble a collection of small, meandering streams going in many directions. One uses determination to converge these streams into a single gentle water flow. When we pull our thoughts together we can return to the inner spring of God which is the source of the water flow and therefore, what is basic to life. In *My Symphony*, William Henry Channing penned: "To live content with small means; to seek elegance rather than luxury, and refinement rather than fashion; to be worthy, not respectable, and wealthy, not rich, to study hard, think quietly, talk gently, act frankly; to listen to stars and birds, to babes and sages, with open heart; to bear all cheerfully, do all bravely, await occasions, hurry never. In a word, to let the spiritual, unbidden and unconscious, grow up through the common." One has no need to search for holiness. It is quite within everyone's grasp.

The Goals

There can be no perseverance without goals. To get to heaven should be the primary goal. It is the reason why each person was created. All other goals, although quite laudable, should not be set in stone because they can be delayed or changed over time. Perseverance offers an alert, forward thinking orientation until a goal is achieved, changed or abandoned. It keeps an individual out of a rut that leads to nowhere and on the move. Perseverance also keeps expectations in balance. They are neither too high, nor too low,

Perseverance: Like a Turtle on the Trail

too many, nor too few. Through planning effectively and doing things as well as possible the golden thread of God's graces and the multicolored threads of goals can form intriguing patterns, some of which could never be imagined.

The mills of God work slowly, but they grind exceedingly fine. To desire a better tomorrow is praiseworthy and should inspire doing good today. Determination holds impetuousness in check. It is challenging to live with problems until such time as they are taken away. Delay does not mean refusal. Perhaps the time is just not right.

> When Thomas Carlyle had finished the first volume of his book, *The French Revolution*, he gave the finished manuscript to his friend John Stuart Mill and asked him to read it. It took Mr. Mill several days to read it and as he read, he realized that it was truly a great literary achievement. Late one night as he finished the last page he laid the manuscript aside by his chair in the den of his home. The next morning the maid came. Seeing those papers on the floor, she thought they were simply discarded; she threw them into the fire, and they were burned.
>
> On March 6, 1835, he never forgot the date, Mill called on Carlyle in deep agony and told him that his work had been destroyed. Carlyle replied, "It's all right. I'm sure I can start over in the morning and do it again."
>
> Finally, after great apologies, John Mill left and started back home. Carlyle watched his friend walking away and said to his wife, "Poor Mill, I feel so sorry for him. I did not want him to see how crushed I really am." Then heaving a sigh, he said, "Well, the manuscript is gone, so I had better start writing again."
>
> It was a long, hard process especially because the inspiration was gone. It is always hard to recapture the verve and the vigor if a man has to do a thing like that twice. But he set out to do it again and finally completed the work.
>
> Thomas Carlyle walked away from disappointment. He could do nothing about a manuscript that was burned up. So it is with us: There are times to get up and get going and let what happened happen.[1]

Sometimes it is a struggle to keep moving when it does not seem like progress is being made. Grace helps to endure without complaining. A person would like to fly, but perhaps he cannot fly because his wings are not yet grown or strong enough. An individual cannot completely rely on his own

---

1. Barclay, *The King and the Kingdom*.

strength, intellect or wit. Total self reliance can easily lead to feeling worn out, distraught or discouraged. A person should try to fly, but gently. Pierre Teilhard de Chardin advises:

> Above all, trust in the slow work of God. We are all, quite naturally, impatient in everything to reach the end without delay. We should like to skip the intermediate stages. We are impatient of being on the way to something unknown, something new. Yet it is the law of all progress that is made by passing through some stages of instability and that it may take a very long time. And so I think it is with you. Your ideas mature gradually. Let them grow. Let them shape themselves without undue haste. Do not try to force them on, as though you could be today what time—that is to say, grace—and circumstances acting on your own good will make you tomorrow. Only God could say what this new Spirit gradually forming within you will be. Give our Lord the benefit of believing that his hand is leading you and accept the anxiety of feeling yourself in suspense and incomplete.[2]

The Driver

A Christian waits with trust that God is working for her good when she does not know how a current situation will turn out, or when things are baffling. She knows who is at the controls and it is not her. God is in the driver's seat and he steers the course of her life. She is in the passenger's seat, and this doesn't mean being the back seat driver. She turned the wheel over to him when she could not go further by her own actions. She is now dependent on divine intervention which is most necessary in a commitment to the excellence of holiness. She no longer prefers the easier, lower level of mediocrity. God assists her in ignoring popular movements and filtering essentials from incidentals. She knows it is always her choice as God respects the freedom and liberty of each person and does not force himself on anyone. Handing the steering wheel over to God is saying yes to him. This becomes a daily habit that goes beyond the call of duty, beyond rules and principles or beyond what is required. She submits to God. And she is surprised. She talks less and listens more, especially at prayer. A job is no longer just something to do to get the bills paid, but something through which love is lived. She finds new insights in routine daily tasks.

---

2. "Prayer of Teilhard de Chardin," quoted at IgnatianSpirituality.com.

She responds with love to aggravations. She is more gracious and smiles more often, even when offended. She takes to heart the words of Louis de Blois:

> In speaking, be circumspect, polite, restrained, and without fault. Love reasonable silence. Do not say things that are utterly vain or useless, and that arouse unbridled laughter.... Avoid excessively sharp and biting words and abominate the vice of detraction and slander.... Also, do not affirm as certain anything that you do not know for sure.... If it should happen that you hear someone saying, mocking or wicked or unkind words, end the conversation, politely, or even modestly and discretely correct the one who was speaking.[3]

The young woman in the passenger's seat looks at her new self, likes what she sees, and resolves that holiness is the real way to go.

Cindy and Brian

The matrimonial covenant between a husband and wife is a very beautiful and unparalleled expression of love. Cindy shares her reflections on this important topic: As a gift of love, sacraments were instituted by Jesus. The *Catechism of the Catholic Church* instructs us that the sacraments are "powers that come forth" from the body of Christ which is ever living and lifegiving. They are actions of the Holy Spirit and "the masterworks of God."

When referencing the highly regarded sacrament of marriage, the catechism officially defines marriage as "a covenant or partnership of life between a man and woman which is ordered to the well being of the spouses and to the procreation and upbringing of children. When validly contracted between two baptized people, marriage is a sacrament." In my experience, marriage is also a state of life, a vocation in which a husband and wife respond to Christ's call to journey together toward eternity in unique closeness and union, each responsible to some extent for the salvation of each other. Through faith and perseverance, spouses rely on the guidance of the Holy Spirit to enable each to help the other to achieve everlasting happiness.

When speaking of marriage, Hartmann and Brickey, in *Journey of Love*, relate, "As we assist each other in overcoming temptations and in

---

3. *Spiritual Works of Louis of Blois*; du Blois, a Benedictine abbot and spiritual writer, who was born at Donstienne, near Liege, in 1506 and died at Liessies in 1566.

sustaining each other in the difficulties of life, we fulfill our own destiny too. We must be in union with each other and with God. As we merge our wills with His we shall proceed joyfully to our eternal goal."

As for my marriage, my husband and I began our journey on a blind date. Not a risk-taker by nature, I hesitated to accept the invitation of mutual friends. However, I really didn't have anything better to do that evening so I resolved to consider the event an adventure. I know now that my non-characteristic response was an inspiration from God, as the outcome of the evening was part of his plan for me.

My date that evening turned out to be a revelation. My husband-to-be was a passionate scientist with a good sense of humor and I enjoyed the evening's conversation which was so different from conversations with my colleagues at the elementary school where I taught. Following this first introductory evening, we began a series of dinners, movies, concerts, and long conversations. Cradle Catholics, we exchanged happy childhood memories and also acknowledged elements of painful dysfunction in both our families.

When he was nine years old, my husband survived the premature death of his father which left an indelible void never filled by his widowed mother and two combative sisters. I was the eldest of five siblings, ranging in age from ten to three years, when my father deserted our family. I became a surrogate parent when my elderly grandmother arrived to run the household as best she could. My mother was thus freed to work three jobs to support us.

The Catholic Church was a safe haven for me. Daily prayer, Mass and the sacraments were and are the treasured practices of my life. For my husband, the Church was a stumbling block, an organization which was somewhat frustrating. Yet, he believed in God and recognized in me a person that God sent to heal and inspire him. He once commented to a friend, "When I learned how much my wife loved a God she could not see, I knew she would be faithful to me who she loved and could see." We agreed that when we married we wanted to create a solid environment, a generational improvement on both sides in which our new family could flourish.

Over time our attraction to each other deepened to become love which we affirmed in God's presence in the Roman Catholic Church in the sacrament of marriage. The Final Blessing, proclaimed in our ceremony was etched upon my heart: "May you live to see your children and your children's children." As God joined us together in one flesh, so were our destinies now entwined forever.

We were married almost a year when we were blessed with our first child, a most welcome son who was joined by a brother and sister in rapid succession. I became a "stay at home mom" for whom days and nights merged as I struggled to keep our home clean and neat and to give our children loving care and individual attention as they progressed from infancy to preschool.

I soon discovered that larger difficulties such as my husband's losing his job for several months were, in reality, more manageable than the day-to-day frustrations of family life—those nitty-gritty moments when tempers flare and patience is lost. How often I paused between laundry and dinner to call upon my silent partner in this marriage, Jesus, who quietly restored me to peace!

Even if all the toys were not in their proper place when my husband came home, I could always depend on a kiss hello and words of encouragement. However, these early years did indeed place some strains on the marital relationship. We learned the hard way that we needed to reserve time to discuss problems such as finding the money to pay for Catholic education and agreeing to forego vacations for this greater good.

It was also very important to reserve time to enjoy our children and to encourage the development of their talents. Many evenings, following dinner, our sons gave us a display of original acrobatic maneuvers and our daughter led us in song. Among my cherished memories is the voice of my oldest son as he began his nighttime prayer: "In the name of the Father and of the Son and of the Gooey Ghost. Amen." (I thank God for the many outcomes of Vatican II, not the least of which was the restoration of the words "Holy Spirit" to the sign of the cross.)

I can still see my five-year-old daughter flitting from one piece of furniture to another, and laughing as she touched them while I prepared her culinary delight—a peanut butter sandwich. "What are you doing?" I asked. "I'm touching God, Mommy. Don't you know he's everywhere?"

As our children progressed to high school, since there were no Catholic high schools available in our area, we entered the public school system. These were happy, hectic years as we moved from football games, wrestling matches, a cappella choir, CCD, band concerts, plays and musicals. I think my husband and I enjoyed these activities all the more due to the burdens of our childhood responsibilities. We never had been given these opportunities for extracurricular activities. Our hearts were filled with gratitude to God whose grace enabled us to provide a healthy family environment so different from the conditions in which we spent our teenage years.

Even though we experienced many dedicated coaches, teachers and strong Christian families, we were challenged at times to live the gospel, even when the world around us seemed deaf to the message. It was hard for our daughter to understand why any of the girls who wore short skirts and plunging necklines to school were among the first to receive prom invitations. Some of our children's classmates engaged in occasional drug use. Concerned about this trend, we were forced, at times, to embarrass our teenagers by calling the parents of classmates having parties to be sure that there would be adequate supervision all evening long. During these tough times, we fought mightily to lead our children beyond compromise for temporary social acceptance or escape.

I recall that one evening at this time my husband took me out to dinner to celebrate our fifteenth wedding anniversary. When our wine glasses were filled, he proposed a toast: "Here's to a perfect marriage!" I was so surprised to hear my husband refer to ours as a perfect marriage! "You know," he continued, "when we were married, we had an idea of perfection which had to change with time. Today my idea of a perfect marriage is one in which we know that nothing can ever come which we cannot surmount together."

Years do fly by! Almost before we knew what was happening, our oldest son graduated from high school. It was then that we searched our souls to free him, an average student, from our preconceived notions that every eighteen-year-old, especially our children, must go to college. He had discovered a talent for woodworking and wanted to go to a technical school where he could become a master carpenter. After some conversation with our partner, Jesus, the master of all carpenters, and his foster father, Joseph, we released our son to fulfill his chosen career. It was hard to pass his empty room each day, but I rejoiced with my husband as our son grew into a well-balanced, successful adult.

As our other children left the comfortable family home in which they had been nurtured, guided and loved we relied on the words of St. Paul: "I planted. Apolos watered. But God gave the growth" (1 Cor 3:6). My husband's parental philosophy became more and more simple: "We may not leave them much money, but we will equip them to serve God in the profession of their choice."

The story does not end here. As the years passed by, I was faced with the hard truth that children do not always fulfill their parents' dreams. One of our sons separated from the Church in which we had reared him. I agonized over his decision because it was my most fervent wish to lead all of our children to Christ in his Church. A family friend, a priest, realized the pain our son's decision caused us. His advice was to remind us that God gave each of us free will. Our son was exerting his right to explore beyond the boundaries I had envisioned. Our job was to remain firm in our own commitment to the Catholic Church, to pray for him, and to continue to love him unconditionally. The fifth Joyful Mystery of the Rosary, "The Finding of the Child Jesus in the Temple," took on deeper meaning for me as I earnestly asked our Blessed Mother to intercede for our son's return to his spiritual home. Although it took years of patience and perseverance, I am grateful that God sent a wonderful Catholic woman, who is now his wife, to lead our son back to his Father's house.

By the time we became "empty nesters," my husband had started his own business, which I thought of as our fourth child. As he lived the American Dream, many long, hard hours claimed his time and energy. I went back to work to assist him in his office. Eventually, we found time for more volunteer work at Church and embraced square dancing for recreation and exercise. One evening, as we finished dinner after a vigorous dance lesson, my husband said, "You know something, dear, the soles of my feet are really hurting. They feel like ground hamburger." What a puzzle that presented to me! When this uncomfortable feeling didn't leave, he sought medical help. The diagnosis took a year which included multiple visits to specialists, painful tests and heartfelt prayer. When the verdict was finally pronounced, we learned that my husband had a rare and incurable form of peripheral neuropathy.

As we entered this final phase of our journey, we were challenged to venture further into the unknown than ever before, led through darkness by the light of faith and God's abundant grace. We persevered through eleven years of my husband's pain, physical deterioration, continual changes in medication (with the accompanying side effects), a cane, a walker, a wheelchair, and ultimately, total disability. During the last year of his life, my husband was totally bedridden and wanted me close to him most of the time. I would make him as comfortable as possible, given his constant pain. Toward evening, when his eyes would slowly close, I would move out to the family room where the tears I hid all day could flow, and my prayers could find words.

There were some high points during those years—joyous weddings, supportive in-laws and the supreme joy of grandchildren—the fulfillment of our marriage blessing. My husband soldiered on and I remained at his side to encourage and strengthen him as the disease took more of him from me every day. Wasn't this what I had vowed on my wedding day? "I will love you and cherish you, in sickness and in health, until death do us part."

Looking back on it now, I see so clearly how God is loving and merciful through it all. My husband and I grew as one through his suffering. He had always been a best friend who expressed his disappointment when I left lights on when they were not needed, but would shrug off occasional damage to the car with, "As long as you are alright, nothing else matters." As his body deteriorated, our spiritual relationship soared. We were soul mates in the truest sense—a precious gift in the midst of combat.

One morning we shared another reading from St. Paul in which we were told that "when the earthly tent we live in is destroyed, we have a building from God, a house not made with hands, eternal in the heavens" (2 Cor 5:1). On that day, my husband looked up at me and said, "I think it's about time to fold up my tent and move on." "My darling," I replied, "God only lent you to us. When the time comes for you to return to him, we will release you reluctantly, but with the utmost confidence. But not one moment sooner than when God calls you home."

A few weeks after this unforgettable moment, my husband's heart began to fail. What had happened on the outside of his body was now invading the inside. I was informed by his primary physician that DNR (do not resuscitate) should be written on his medical records and should be my instruction to all his doctors when he could no longer speak for himself. The thought of having to discontinue my beloved husband's life support was more than I could bear. Through my tears, I reminded God that I had never asked Him to take my husband. I believed in redemptive suffering and wanted every soul God had reserved for my husband's sacrifices to be saved. However at this moment, at this crossroads, I asked God to be the one who would make the decision when it was time for my husband to return to Him.

About a month later, my husband died in his sleep. I like to think that he settled down on earth that evening and woke up with Jesus. I honor his memory each day through prayer and continued ministry in our parish. Our children and grandchildren are conduits of God's love and my husband's love to me. As they grow, there are subtle reminders of their father and grandfather—one is fascinated by turtles, another's eyes sparkle when he tells a story, just like his grandfather's. It is apparent that my husband's presence abides in those he loved and those who will always love him. I live on in peace. I have learned that although love may be pushed to its limits through the trials of life, truly, love never ends for those who persevere.

> It's rough, it's tough, it's work.
> Anybody who says it isn't
> Has never been married.
> Marriage has far bigger problems
> Than toothpaste squeezed
> From the middle of the tube.
>
> Marriage means . . .
> Grappling, aching, struggling.
> It means putting up
> With personality weaknesses
> Accepting criticism
> And giving each other freedom to fail.
> It means sharing deep feelings
> About fear and rejection.
> It means turning self pity into laughter
> And taking a walk to gain control.
>
> Marriage means . . .
> Gentleness and joy
> Toughness and fortitude
> Fairness and forgiveness
> And a walloping amount of sacrifice.
>
> Marriage means . . .
> Learning when to say nothing
> When to keep talking
> When to push a little
> When to back off.

It means acknowledging
"I can't be God to you—
I need Him, too."

Marriage means . . .
You are the other part of me
I am the other part of you.
We'll work though
With never a thought of walking out.

Marriage means . . .
Two imperfect mates
Building permanently
Giving totally
In partnership with a perfect God.

~Ruth Harms Calkin
"Love Is So Much More, Lord"

The Key

Mahatma Gandhi said: "Prayer is the key that unlocks the door of the morning and locks the door of the evening." Francois Millet (1814–1875), a naturalist painter, painted simple themes of everyday nineteenth-century French country life. Perhaps his most famous work was *The Angelus* which shows a peasant farmer husband and wife in a field, pausing to reverently pray the Angelus as they hear the bell ring in the distant church. This painting reflects quiet moments to honor God's presence in the midst of hard days. These prayerful moments help to make the day holy. The Angelus, earnestly said, will keep us close to God and help us to obtain Divine aid. Commonly said at dawn, noon and dusk, this prayer honors the Incarnation by recalling to mind the Angel Gabriel's visit to Mary. The practice of saying three Hail Marys in honor of the Incarnation was introduced by the Franciscans in 1263. A three-verse addition first appeared in the mid-sixteenth century. The verses as known today appeared before the second decade of the seventeenth century

We must keep asking God for final perseverance. In John 16:23 Jesus said, "I give you my assurance whatever you ask the Father, he will give you

Perseverance: Like a Turtle on the Trail

in my name." Jesus will help us to persevere. It would be a gracious gesture to honor his Incarnation and his assistance with perseverance by saying a daily Angelus. This will keep Christians attentive to what is truly important. Perseverance fosters a humility that has a deep knowledge and appreciation of the goodness and providence of God. Prayer brings to light the basic realities of the spiritual life. Christians who live a fast paced life need to step back and realize holiness is not an option. It is a responsibility. Prayer is the connection to holiness. Prayer not only is the key that opens the door of the morning, it is also the key that opens the door to many incomprehensible graces. God has blessed humankind with the precious gift of freedom of choice. May we persevere in making decisions that reflect Jesus' love as we walk in grace on the holiness path.

> The Angel of the Lord declared unto Mary
> And she conceived of the Holy Spirit.
>
> Hail Mary . . .
>
> Behold the handmaid of the Lord
> Be it done unto me according to your word.
>
> Hail Mary . . .
>
> And the Word was made Flesh
> And dwelt among us.
>
> Hail Mary . . .
>
> Pray for us, O holy Mother of God
> That we may be made worthy of the promises of Christ.
>
> Let us pray

Pour forth, we beseech you, O Lord, your grace into our hearts, that we to whom the Incarnation of Christ, your Son, was made known by the message of an Angel, may, by his passion and cross, be brought to the glory of his resurrection through the same Christ our Lord. Amen

Joy: Inside a Christian Heart

IT SEEMS THERE ARE three general categories of joy. Natural joy happens in time. It is not a constant condition, but rather a feeling that lifts us up for awhile and comes from looking forward to something good, obtaining something good, or enjoying something that is a result of a basic good. There is joy in doing the right thing. There is joy in completing a task we have been avoiding because it is displeasing to us. There is joy that results from the hard work of earning a college degree. We experience joy through our senses. We are delighted at the sight of natural beauty, we are uplifted by the sound of a symphony. We relish the taste of good food. We are comforted by the feel of a soft beloved teddy bear. We are refreshed by the scent of spring flowers. Natural joy can come from a planned activity or come out of the blue for no apparent reason whatsoever.

Far deeper and richer a gift, however, is supernatural joy. This is a joy that is linked to the eternal. No person has this joy unless he or she prays to God and lives in a way that honors what he teaches. Joy in one's lifestyle is the hallmark that reveals God's presence and witnesses Christ's resurrection. Christian joy is a gift from God that sustains us through the good and bad circumstances in life and accompanies us to the fullness of joy in the heavenly kingdom. Bonaventure tells us: "In God alone is there primordial and true delight, and in all our delights it is this delight that we are seeking."

The fullness of Divine joy cannot be experienced on this earth. It is ours when we reach heaven and enjoy the beatific vision. No one can adequately explain it. We cannot even imagine it. It is written, "The eye has not seen, nor ear heard, neither has it entered into the heart of man, what things God has prepared for them that love him" (1 Cor 2:9). This is the joy that has no end.

Happiness and joy are sometimes thought of as similar feelings. They are often used interchangeably. Happiness is expressed in smiles and laughter, and comes from something good that happens to us. Happiness alternates with other feelings. It is a pleasant occurrence, but can be taken away in an instant.

Christian joy resides in the depths of the soul, and is more than pleasure or happiness. It evokes a nameless yearning for something more than this earth can offer and it comes with prerequisites. We must communicate with God, obey his teachings and live with the intentions of pleasing him. Christian joy is not limited to positive emotions. It is more a by-product of knowing and living God's truth.

Usually not an experience like brightly colored fireworks, Christian joy is more like a serene inner glow. Perhaps an individual can visualize it as a tranquil deep lake hidden at the bottom of the soul. When difficulties are overwhelming, one seeks refuge by submerging into its placid, clear, restorative water. With the help of divine grace, an individual rises up refreshed and invigorated, ready to face challenges with peace and faith. The water of grace illuminates and transforms our spiritual landscape so that we can manage whatever life has in store. Life on the spiritual landscape proves that we need God, we need the Church, and there are no substitutes. To be spiritual is to grow in friendship with God, to be a sign of the eternal realm, and to live in love rather than fear. Isn't Christian joy more evident when we act out of love for our convictions rather than act out of fear of punishment? Problems should purify people as prayer draws them closer to the reality for which they were created. Anselm of Canterbury knew this, stating: "I have not yet thought or said, O Lord, how much your blessed ones will rejoice. Surely, they will rejoice in the degree that they will love. And they will love in the degree that they will know. How much will they know you in that day, Lord, how much will they love you?"

Singing Birds

> This seems a cheerful world, Donatus, when I view it from this fair garden, under the shadow of these vines. But if I climbed some great mountain and looked out over the wide lands, you know very well what I would see—brigands on the high roads, pirates on the seas; in the amphitheatres men murdered to please applauding crowds; under all roofs misery and selfishness. It is really a bad world, Donatus, an incredibly bad world. Yet in the midst of it I have found a quiet and holy people. They have discovered a joy which is a thousand times better than any pleasures of this sinful life. They are despised and persecuted, but they care not.

They have overcome the world. These people, Donatus, are the Christians—and I am one of them.[1]

Jesus is the center of Christian joy. The joy Jesus offers is found in abiding in him. This type of abiding is like a spring deep down inside that never runs dry no matter what happens. Abide means to live in a place permanently. It is a singular grace to abide in the Heart of Jesus. Christian joy originates from his Heart and remains alive in us by our prayer, worship, reception of the sacraments, good works and living in the light of eternal salvation. Jesus is the perfection of lasting joy and the goal of being a Christian. Jesus is the only person who can give the total fullness of joy because he is the only one who completely fills deepest human needs, desires and longings.

Wonder and joy are closely related. A lovely dimension of the present moment is a joyful wonder. This quality is neither a remembrance of a past joy nor anticipation of a future joy. It occurs unexpectedly like bubbles of pure delight. When it is gone, there is rarely a reason to dwell on its passing or speculate on its return. To be surprised by joy is to feel it in the pleasure of the moment. Wouldn't it be delightful to have a "wonder" shelf in a quiet corner of our home? A family member who is creative could place one object of wonder on an empty shelf and change that object periodically. Objects can be as varied as snowflakes: a seashell, a rock, a feather, a toy that doesn't need batteries or electricity, a picture of a loved one, tree, or mountain, a poem, statue of a saint, holy card, Sacred Heart badge or anything else that gives us a sense of awe. A person spends a few moments pondering what is in it that attracts and delights him or her about the object. It is a time for wonder, far far away from any intellectual evaluation or scholarly interpretation.

Authentic joy is not a stimulant that causes us to laugh and sing in the happiness of the present. Rather, it is a deep contentment in knowing that God truly loves us and wants us to be with him in heaven. Believing in the goodness of God helps to envision each day as a gift with a new resurrection and life as a beautiful part of his creation.

"Darkness bursts to glory, and its silence breaks to song. The flaming dawn shouts gladness with a joy that always sings and lifts us soaring to the sky like a bird with outspread wings. He pours himself to emptiness in the mystery of sweet song; his canticle of loveliness exultingly he sends beyond the clouds and sunshine to where the rainbow ends. All spent, his voice is silent I am alone without a song; and sorrow it is timeless: sorrow, it is

---

1. Cyprian, as quoted in Renfree, *Beyond the Horizon*.

long. For loneliness cuts deeply as cuts no other thing, but I know with each tomorrow, a bird will always sing!"[2]

Like Little Children

Jesus said, "Unless you are like little children you will not enter the Kingdom of Heaven." It is a lovely grace to see with the eyes of little children. The joy of a child is simple and beautiful. Questions disappear as they are replaced by wonder. God will take care of things if problems and questions are placed in his heart. A childlike joy goes beyond the confines of the mind, and basks in the awe of the heart. A child's joy is open and honest. With humility, we too can bow to the mystery of God. Trust opens our heart so that we can hold on tight to God when unexplainable darkness surrounds us. A sustaining joy moves us past the circumstances of life and fixes our eyes on God. We are encouraged by Teresa of Calcutta: "The best way to show your gratitude to God and people is to accept everything with joy. A joyful heart is a normal result of a heart burning with love. Joy is strength. Let nothing so disturb us, so fill us with sorrow or discouragement, as to make us forfeit the joy of the resurrection. Joy is not simply a matter of temperament in the service of God and souls; it is always hard. All the more reason why we should try to acquire it and make it grow in our hearts. We may not be able to give much, but we can always give the joy that springs from a heart that is in love with God."

Children teach us with their light hearted joy. They fight and a few minutes later they are friends again. They laugh at themselves. They build a sand castle at the shore. A wave comes in and washes it away. They laugh and rebuild. A childlikeness delights in new beginnings. Just for fun, we should make a joy list and add to it every day. What gives us joy? Why, if we look, joy is all around us: Bright red geraniums, a full moon, bread baking in the oven, a warm fire on a cold night, raindrops on roses....

Christian joy is usually unaffected by external circumstances because it is a prayerful focus of the heart. True Christian joy is more refined than "felt" joy. Rather, it is a deep, settled commitment, secured in God, bonded in hope and lived by Christian principles. It is our anchor in this swirling sea of life. This disposition does not demand that a person is perpetually cheerful. Common sense says this is not real. The sacred is experienced in

---

2. Holy card printed by Discalced Carmelite nuns, Carmelite Monastery, Terre Haute Indiana.

normal everyday ups and downs of life. God is found all around us, from the monastery to the mortuary, from the corner church to the corner cafe. John Paul II realized this better than most: "There is no law which lays it down that you must smile. But you can make a gift of your smile; you can be the heaven of kindness in your family." Kindness is what God's love looks like in practice.

Have Confidence

Christian joy is based on our confidence in being a daughter or son of God who loves us tenderly and will never leave us. Evelyn Underhill once wrote: "This is the secret of joy. We will no longer strive for our own way; but commit ourselves, easily and simply, to God's way, acquiesce in his will and in so doing find our peace." This is possible when prayer is an all important daily commitment. Intentional prayer is the proof that we believe in God's particular and unique love for us. He is the only one who will always be there for us. God loves us as surely as he loved his own son. Because his love is unchanging and consistent, it is possible for us to trust him in all circumstances. Our joy in God develops from heartfelt prayer, deep faith and a yearning for his intimacy. Because God loves us unreservedly, our love for God must be constant. This happens when our prayer is consistent because love, as a discipline of the mind, is the product of prayer. Good prayer helps us give away love. Teresa of Calcutta reminds everyone how to love: "Give love to your children, your wife or husband, to a next door neighbor. Let no one ever come to you without leaving better or happier. Be the living expression of God's kindness; kindness in your face; kindness in your eyes; kindness in your smile; kindness in your warm greeting." Indeed, love honors every person, even though we may completely disagree with him or her.

Sabeth

"Since my childhood I have brought all my joys and sorrows to our Lord." Wise words from Elizabeth Catez, also known as Elizabeth of the Trinity. Who was this young French woman whose greatest joy was to know the gift of God? The Carmel in Terre Haute gives us this brief description of her life:

Elizabeth Catez, known to her family and friends as "Sabeth," was born July 18, 1880, near Bourges, France, the daughter of a military officer. Early in her life, the family moved to Dijon where, at the age of seven, she lost her father. Under the firm guidance of her mother, Elizabeth, a vivacious and strong willed child, learned to master her temper and moderate her natural impulsivity. By her eleventh year, when she made her First Communion, she had acquired a degree of self possession unusual for a child her age. A visit to the Carmel in Dijon on that memorable day gave her the key to her name, Elizabeth, "house of God," and was the beginning of her orientation to the mystery of God dwelling within her.

Both she and her sister, Marguerite, two years her junior, pursued a course of musical studies at the Conservatory of Music in Dijon, and at the age of thirteen, the talented Elizabeth won first prize in a piano contest. Elizabeth's vibrant sensitivity as an artist and her affectionate nature made her an enthusiastic and lively companion to her many friends and admirers. Yet her attraction to interior prayer had been developing during these years of adolescence and at the age of seventeen, she asked her mother's permission to enter Carmel. Mme. Catez delayed for two years, even forbidding her any contact with the Carmelite nuns, but she withdrew that prohibition within a short time. Elizabeth endured this postponement with docility, learning to live in the presence of God, whether in the midst of her family, or in a whirl of social activities. Eventually her mother, seeing Elizabeth's unwavering attraction to the cloister, consented that she might become a Carmelite when she was twenty-one. In spite of the keen pain she felt at leaving her mother and sister, Elizabeth hastened to answer the call she had heard in her heart since the age of fourteen and entered her beloved Carmel on August 2, 1901, only two weeks after her twenty-first birthday.

From the beginning, Elizabeth's Carmelite life was marked by her inward attraction to silence, where she, the musician, became a passionate and sensitive "listener" to the Word who spoke so secretly in her heart. After a year in Carmel she wrote, "I should like to be utterly silent, entirely adoring so as to penetrate into him more and more, and become so full of him that I shall be able to give him by prayer to those poor souls who do not know the gift of God." Not only was her prayer itself an apostolate, but she also knew from experience that it was possible, even in a busy and active life, to live continually in the presence of God. Hers was no sterile solitude, nor did her spirit of recollection isolate her from the daily concerns of community life. Rather, she found Christ everywhere and every activity immersed her more in God.

Yet, Elizabeth also experienced her own weakness and her inability to maintain peace of heart by her own efforts. "I, too, need to go in search of my Master who hides himself well, but then I rouse up my faith and I am more pleased not to enjoy his presence, so that he may enjoy my love." Faith became for her the light that guided her most surely through the fluctuations that afflict the human spirit in its journey to union with God. Her own struggles made her compassionate toward the sufferings of others, and as she discovered the depths and grandeur of her vocation, she spontaneously shared it with a large group of correspondents, most of them lay persons. "It seems to me that I have found my heaven on earth because heaven is God, and God is in my soul. The day I understood this, everything became clear to me, and I would like to proclaim this secret aloud to those whom I love, so that they also may always cling to God in everything."

Profoundly influenced by the great saints of Carmel, Teresa of Jesus, John of the Cross, and Therese of the Child Jesus, Elizabeth, nevertheless, turned more and more to the scriptures for the nourishment of her life in Christ. It was primarily in the Epistles of St. Paul that she found the pattern of her personal vocation traced out. There she learned that she had been "chosen in Christ before the foundation of the world . . . and appointed to live for the praise of his glory." This phrase became her "new name" as she set herself to the task of becoming a "Praise of Glory" of the Holy Trinity. She wrote: "A Praise of Glory is a soul that dwells in God, loves him with a love that is pure and disinterested . . . a silent soul, which remains like a lyre beneath the mysterious touch of the Holy Spirit . . . a soul that gazes steadfastly upon God in faith and simplicity."

This thought preoccupied Elizabeth until the end of her life, but as the effects of Addison's disease made themselves felt in increasing fatigue, her spiritual insight deepened. She realized that God had also chosen her to be "conformed to the image of his Son" and that this meant "sharing his sufferings and becoming like to him in his death." For this was not a gloomy prospect but one full of light, even though it required heroic faith and self forgetfulness as her strength ebbed away and she knew only hours of pain. Elizabeth's last months, tortured as they were, were marked by a constant charity and consideration for her community, her family, and her friends. During that period of extraordinary fruitfulness, she wrote four spiritual "treastises" and seventy eight letters overflowing with affection for those she was leaving behind. She died on November 9, 1906, after five brief years in Carmel.[3]

Elizabeth's mother said that as a child Elizabeth delighted in talking. She was a cheerful and generous chatterbox. Her playmates saw her as warm and friendly. Elizabeth delighted in the bustle, parades, sham cavalry fights and military bands of her youth. As a young teen, she was vivacious and charming. Her piano artistry won admiration and praise. She was lively, ardent and passionate. In her late teens, she led an active social life attending parties and enjoying them all. She loved beautiful clothes, liked to play tennis and croquet, and enjoyed fine dining. She participated in impromptu music sessions, enjoyed sewing lessons and relished the beauty of the mountains, sea, sky, and all of nature on trips she took with her mother and sister.

During her teens, Elizabeth found much joy in her life but she longed for a deeper joy that she could only find in Carmel. Her spiritual life was highly developed before she entered Carmel. When she was a postulant, everything delighted her. Her cheerful and spontaneous writing revealed a deep spiritual peace in reference to drudgery, sickness and death.

Elizabeth is a modern spiritual teacher who illustrates how joy requires living in peace. Because peace begins with ourselves, we must make a decision each day to live from joy inherent in our union with the Triune God. We are helped with this decision by Julian of Norwich: "The greatest honor that you can give to Almighty God, greater than all your penances and sacrifices and mortifications, is to live joyfully because of the knowledge of his love." Only by loving and being loved by God, do we have the great freedom to be ourselves, to blossom, and to savor our moments of grace. This freedom flows beneath the feasts and famines of our days because our constant in life is God and his love.

We might want to record our moments, or even simple stories, of grace in a "moments of grace" journal. They would basically be small things that we would tend to forget, a description of a bird building a nest, clouds floating across the sky, or a child at play.

The journal would be an inexpensive notebook, something like Therese used when she wrote *Story of a Soul*. How refreshing it would be to

---

3. From a pamphlet printed by the Discalced Carmelite nuns, Carmelite Monastery, Terre Haute, Indiana. Elizabeth was beatified by Pope John Paul II on November 25, 1984. She was canonized a saint by Pope Francis on October 16, 2016.

reflect upon our moments of grace years after they happened. Contents in this journal would be precious gifts to keep or to share with others.

Prayer helps us live in the company of Jesus and strive to see all people as human beings created by God. Problems are then opportunities to collaborate with God, choosing joy each day, and in so doing being liberated from the constraints of negativity. Deep Christian joy, that blossoms from the heart and is shared with others, fosters a common unity and purpose. This is evident when we share aspects of our Catholic faith as Augustine knew: "When many men rejoice together, there is a richer joy in each individual, since they enkindle themselves and they inflame one another."

Jesus empowers us with his serenity in the midst of personal trials. This is why joy is the greatest sign of God's presence. The lifeline with Jesus is prayer which increases our awareness of his expansive presence. Often, we put off praying until we feel the time or our disposition, is right. However, there is no right mood for prayer. Having distractions or inappropriate thoughts during prayer does not mean we are praying poorly, but rather that we are being faithful to the discipline of daily prayer. Prayer is thus an act of the will wherein we desire to give all our confused thoughts and problems to God. Too much reflection on the negatives in our past wears us down and erodes the joy of the present. We should therefore leave the past to God's mercy, living instead in the present. The same holds true for the future: for if we allow the past or future to crash into the present they invariably tarnish the grace and sacrament of the present moment. The spirit of joy requires discipline of the mind. We need to control our wandering thoughts and try as best we can to enjoy life in the gift of today. If we altruistically love our neighbor, we are active conduits of God's love.

Perfect Joy

Most of us need the encouragement that comes from joy. However, the saints among us can live the reality of joy without the need to feel its wonder. This story illustrates perfect joy and is taken from *The Little Flowers of St. Francis*, or the "*Fioretti*."

> One winter day Francis, who is the saint of joy, was coming to St. Mary of the Angels from Perugia with Brother Leo, and the bitter cold made them suffer keenly. Francis called to Brother Leo, who was walking a bit ahead of him, and he said: "Brother Leo, even if the Friars Minor in every country give a great example of holiness

and integrity and good edification, nevertheless write down and note carefully that perfect joy is not in that."

When he had walked on a bit, Francis called him again, saying: "Brother Leo, even if a Friar Minor gives sight to the blind, heals the paralyzed, drives out devils, gives hearing back to the deaf, makes the lame walk, and restores speech to the dumb, and what is still more, brings back to life a man who has been dead four days, write that perfect joy is not in that."

Going on further, Francis cried out again in a strong voice: "Brother Leo, if a Friar Minor knew all languages and all sciences and Scripture, if he also knew how to prophesy and to reveal not only the future but also the secrets of the consciences and minds of others, write down and note carefully that perfect joy is not in that."

As they continued to walk, Francis called again forcefully: "Brother Leo, Little Lamb of God, even if a Friar Minor could speak with the voice of an angel, and knew the courses of the stars and the powers of herbs, and knew all about the treasures in the earth, and if he knew the qualities of birds and fishes, animals, humans, roots, trees, rocks, and waters, write down and note carefully that true joy is not in that."

Going on a bit farther, Francis called again strongly: "Brother Leo, even if a Friar Minor could preach so well that he should convert all infidels to the faith of Christ, write that perfect joy is not there."

Now when he had been talking this way for a distance of two miles, Brother Leo in great amazement asked him: "Father, I beg you in God's name to tell me where perfect joy is."

Francis replied: "When we come to St. Mary of the Angels, soaked by the rain and frozen by the cold, all soiled with mud and suffering from hunger, and we ring at the gate of the place and the brother porter comes and says angrily: 'Who are you?' And we say: 'We are two of your brothers.' And he contradicts us, saying: 'You are not telling the truth. Rather you are two rascals who go around deceiving people and stealing what they give to the poor. Go away!' And he does not open for us, but makes us stand outside in the snow and rain, cold and hungry, until night falls—then if we endure all those insults and cruel rebuffs patiently, without being troubled and without complaining, and if we reflect humbly and charitably that that porter really knows us and that God makes him speak against us, oh, Brother Leo, write that perfect joy is there."

"And if we continue to knock, and the porter comes out in anger, and drives us away with curses and hard blows like bothersome scoundrels, saying; 'Get away from here, you dirty thieves—go to the hospital! Who do you think you are? You certainly won't eat or sleep here'—and if we bear it patiently and take the insults with joy and love in our hearts, Oh, Brother Leo, write that that is perfect joy!"

"And if later, suffering intensely from hunger and the painful cold, with night falling, we still knock and call, and crying loudly beg him to open for us and let us come in for the love of God, and he grows still more angry and says: 'Those fellows are bold and shameless ruffians. I'll give them what they deserve.' And he comes out with a knotty club, and grasping us by the cowl throws us onto the ground, rolling us in the mud and snow, and beats us with that club so much that he covers our bodies with wounds—if we endure all those evils and insults and blows with joy and patience, reflecting that we must accept and bear the sufferings of the Blessed Christ patiently for love of Him, oh, Brother Leo, write: that is perfect joy!"

"And now hear the conclusion, Brother Leo. Above all the graces and gifts of the Holy Spirit which Christ gives to his friends is that of conquering oneself and willingly enduring sufferings, insults, humiliations, and hardships for the love of Christ. For we cannot glory in all those other marvelous gifts of God, as they are not ours but God's, as the Apostle says: 'What have you that you have not received?' But we can glory in the cross of tribulations and afflictions, because that is ours, and so the Apostle says: 'I will not glory save in the Cross of Our Lord Jesus Christ.'"

Francis accepted suffering in the way of the Beatitudes. In his Sermon on the Mount, Jesus explained how poor, hungry, mourning and suffering people are tenderly loved by God, blessed by God because they hope in God despite overwhelming circumstances. Although they were not highly blessed on earth, they would be highly blessed in heaven. Francis makes very real that perfect joy does not come from many talents and abilities, since these are never ultimately ours, but are gifts from God. Francis, therefore, believed that the only really true gifts we can give God, which are not originally from God, are our sufferings.

On the natural level we, of course, do not want suffering in our life but, having reached the state described in the Beatitudes, we can accept suffering with joy. Instead of trying to avoid pain and trials, we can accept them in a spirit that would allow us to offer this rarely appreciated human gift back to God. This is the cause of Francis's perfect joy: he found the only thing that he had which he could give back to the Lord. This is how to live the Beatitudes, how to live on a supernatural level. We are then able to say: "I will not glory, save in the Cross of our Lord Jesus Christ." Perfect joy is found in fidelity, consistency in prayer and patiently enduring the gifts we give to God. Joy is an interior state independent from that which affects us externally. For beneath all the hardships is the fundamental reality of joy. The background to all suffering is total faith in the ultimate triumph of the cross of Christ.

> Joyful, joyful, we adore you, God of glory, Lord of love;
> Hearts unfold like flow'rs before you, Op'ning to the sun above.
> Melt the clouds of sin and sadness; Drive the dark of doubt away;
> Giver of immortal gladness, Fill us with the light of day!
>
> All your works with joy surround you, Earth and heav'n reflect your rays,
> Stars and angels sing around you, Center of unbroken praise;
> Field and forest, vale and mountain, Flow'ry meadow, flashing sea,
> Chanting bird and flowing fountain, Praising you eternally!
>
> Always giving and forgiving, Ever blessing, ever blest,
> Wellspring of the joy of living, Ocean depth of happy rest!
> Loving Father, Christ our brother, Let your light upon us shine;
> Teach us how to love each other, Lift us to the joy divine.
>
> Mortals, join the mighty chorus, Which the morning stars began;
> God's own love is reigning o'er us, Joining people hand in hand.
> Ever singing, march we onward, Victors in the midst of strife;
> Joyful music lifts us sunward, In the triumph song of life.
>
> ~Henry van Dyke

Eucharistia: Holy Adoration

"We stopped in at the cathedral for a few minutes; and, while we looked around in respectful silence, a woman carrying a market basket came in and knelt down in one of the pews to pray briefly. This was something entirely new to me. To the synagogues or to the Protestant churches which I had visited, one went only for services. But here was someone interrupting her everyday shopping errands to come into this church, although no other person was in it, as though she were here for an intimate conversation. I could never forget that."[1]

A very beautiful sign of growth within the Catholic Church is an increase in Eucharistic Adoration. There are more opportunities than ever before to participate in weekly, monthly or perpetual exposition of the Blessed Sacrament in our churches. Immeasurable spiritual graces can be drawn from this singular gift.

Catholic Christians grow in holiness through a deeper understanding, and therefore have a greater appreciation, of Christ in the Eucharist. Jesus transforms each person into becoming one with him and with each other. Spending time with Jesus keeps water from the spring of grace flowing through the Church, world and ourselves. We are graced with wisdom from Teresa of Calcutta: "Each time we look upon Jesus in the Blessed Sacrament, he raises us up into deeper union with himself, opens up the floodgates of his merciful love to the whole world and brings us closer to the day of his final victory 'where every knee will bend and proclaim Jesus Christ as Lord.'" The Eucharistic presence provides all Catholics with the perfect place to pray.

> Dark is the church, and dim the worshippers,
> Hushed with bowed heads as though by some old spell,

---

1. Stein, *Life in a Jewish Family*, 401.

Eucharistia: Holy Adoration

> While through the incense laden air there stirs
> The admonition of a silver bell.
>
> Dark is the church, save where the altar stands,
> Dressed like a bride, illustrious with light,
> Where one old priest exalts with tremulous hands
> The one true solace of man's fallen plight. . . .
>
> ~Ernest Dawson
> Benedictio Domini v. 2, 3

Prayers with the Blessed Sacrament are as varied as flowers in a field. Prayers may be from printed sources, from memory, or from a spontaneous impulse. We pray the Liturgy of the Hours, rosary, litanies and novenas. Whatever the source, prayers are signs of love for Jesus. Devotion to Jesus is also a reminder that there are many people who do not love him. They may be rich in material possessions but starving spiritually. There are also many poor people who are likewise indifferent to Jesus. To keep those people in prayer is an important and beautiful way to help bring about true peace on earth. The words of Peter of Alcantara open one's eyes: "Our Lord in the Blessed Sacrament has his hands full of graces and he is ready to bestow them on anyone who asks for them." We abide in Jesus and in that abiding, pray for our own needs and the needs of all humankind. Problems may seem overwhelming, but Christ's presence in the Eucharist will be sustaining during the most severe of trials. One should not be afraid to ask for the desires of the heart. After he was ordained, Archbishop Fulton Sheen spent a holy hour in the presence of the Blessed Sacrament each day. He believed that, "The holy hour becomes like an oxygen tank to revive the breath of the Holy Spirit in the midst of the foul and fetid atmosphere of the world." We pray intercessory prayers as a response to our love for God and for his people.

> Watch, dear Lord,
> With those who wake,
> Or watch, or weep tonight,
> And give your angels and saints charge
> Over those who sleep.
> Tend your sick ones, O Lord Christ,
> Rest your weary ones,
> Bless your dying ones,

> Soothe your suffering ones,
> Pity your afflicted ones,
> Shield your joyous ones,
> And all for your love's sake
> Amen
>
> ~Augustine

A singularly beautiful prayer to pray in Jesus' presence is the breviary or the Liturgy of the Hours. Since this is the official universal prayer of the Church, those who pray it are deeply bonded with this worldwide Church. The Liturgy of the Hours is a tangible link with all who hold the same book in their hands and for all of humanity for whom the prayers are said. The Liturgy of the Hours is an everyday anchor, reassurance, companion, and source of praise and thanksgiving. The Catholic is praying in the name of the Church; he prays with her and for her in adoration, contrition, thanksgiving and supplication. Catholics mark the same pages, follow the same seasons, and change volumes according to the liturgical calendar. The Liturgy of the Hours unites all those who are praying it at whatever time of day or night, like gentle waves that keep moving as the world is turning. Catholics pray for the whole of humanity as they stand before God as brothers and sisters, intrinsically connected to every person in the world. Some pray Morning Prayer and know others are praying Midday Prayer and still others Evening Prayer in different time zones. Imagine the myriad of graces that descend upon the whole of humanity as an individual quietly prays the Liturgy of the Hours in Jesus' presence, alone in a quiet church. There are so many graces bestowed of which the solitary praying person is unaware.

A Worthy Habit

Regular Eucharistic adoration draws a person into the need for silence. The more one is silent before God, the more she realizes how silence is necessary to balance daily noise. There is so much confusion, heartache and bewilderment in today's society which confirms the great need for silent adoration of Jesus in the host. Alphonsus Liguori, who wrote a whole book on visits to the Blessed Sacrament, urges people forward: "Withdraw yourself from people and spend at least a quarter of an hour or a half hour in some church in the presence of the Blessed Sacrament. Taste and see how sweet is the Lord, and you will learn from your own experience how many graces this will bring to you." Eucharistic adoration nourishes faith in ways that cannot possibly be understood or envisioned. To have Jesus present with humanity until the end of time is a singular honor. A young woman leaves the clamor and hurry of secular society behind as she crosses the threshold of the church, the house of God. She enters the sacred sanctuary and kneels before Jesus in the Blessed Sacrament. The psalmist said: "Be still and know that I am God." This hallowed refuge makes those words ring true. The toil and distractions of the day are released as the quiet of God is embraced. Prayer is the deepest expression of who a person is as a human being. It fortifies the soul, and fills deep needs in these anxious times. "Because Christ himself is present in the sacrament of the altar, he is to be honored with the worship of adoration. 'To visit the Blessed Sacrament is . . . a proof of gratitude, an expression of love, and a duty of adoration toward Christ our Lord.'"[2]

> Joy, beauty, awe, supermost worship blending
> In one long breath of perfect ecstasy,
> Song from our hearts to God's own heart ascending
> The mortal merged in immortality.
>
> There veiled beneath that sacramental whiteness,
> The wonder that all wonders doth transcend,
> The word that kindled chaos into brightness,
> Our Lord, our God, our origin, our end.
>
> Light, light, a sea of light, unshored, supernal,
> Is all about our finite being spread,
> Deep, soundless waves of harmonies eternal
> Their balm celestial on our spirits shed.
>
> O Source of Life! O Fount of waters living!
> O Love, to whom all powers of mind and soul,
> We give, and find again within the giving,
> Of thee renewed, made consecrate and whole.
>
> ~Eleanor Rogers Cox
> "At Benediction"

---

2. Paul VI, MF66 (CCC 1418).

Eucharistic Adoration is not always easy. Sometimes a person is very aware of Jesus' presence and sometimes not. If an individual is experiencing difficulties, he takes courage. Therese of Lisieux is very supportive: "Kneeling before the tabernacle, I can think of only one thing to say to our Lord: 'My God, you know that I love you.' And I feel that my prayer does not weary Jesus knowing my weakness, he is satisfied with my good will." To experience holy or positive feelings is not significant. The important thing is that we are there loving Jesus in spite of ourselves. We never find ourselves by seeking ourselves, but by finding ourselves in Jesus. To see Jesus as gift in the tabernacle or monstrance is to be more sensitive to the movements of God within humanity. At this point one treats others as gifts. Ego enhancers are not the source of authenticity because they cannot authentically fill the emptiness within. Regular time with the Blessed Sacrament proves only God can do that. We are guided by Teresa of Calcutta: "The time you spend with Jesus in the Blessed Sacrament is the best time you will spend on earth. Each moment that you spend with Jesus will deepen your union with him and make your soul everlastingly more glorious and beautiful in heaven." An unknown author gives this advice: "Be still. Be silent, alone, and empty before your God. Say nothing, ask nothing and be silent. Let your God look upon you. That is all. He knows. He understands. He loves you with an enormous love. He only wants to look upon you with his love. Quiet. Be still. Let your God love you!"

True Happiness

Listen to the words of Benedict XVI: "Dear young people, the happiness you are seeking, the happiness you have a right to enjoy, has a name and a face: It is Jesus of Nazareth, hidden in the Eucharist. Only he gives the fullness of life to humanity! Be completely convinced of this: Christ takes from you nothing that is beautiful and great, but brings everything to perfection for the glory of God, the happiness of men and women, and the salvation of the world."

Far from any sentiment, magic or mystical visions, Jesus' presence calls again and again. He is the best teacher and greatest confidant. There is no need for masks or illusions. Jesus is the force that keeps Christians moving ahead. He guides people to the full flowering of their lives

Adoration keeps the heart door open so one can see Jesus' love inside the heart, and just as important his love in the hearts of others. Embracing

Eucharistia: Holy Adoration

Jesus' presence during adoration must coincide with embracing his presence in others, from dear ones to strangers. All are bound to God, to his Church and to one another in the Eucharist. This provides liberation from worry and fear because it develops a greater trust in God's mercy and love and a greater trust in the goodness of others. Teresa of Calcutta directs us: "Never let anyone come to you without coming away better and happier. Everyone should see goodness in your face, in your eyes, in your smile." Many are longing for an authentic spiritual life, and it is up to us to lead them to this life, which is only found in Christ. Embracing his presence at adoration allows an individual to live his presence by finding goodness everywhere. Believing that Jesus is present in the Blessed Sacrament leads to reverence for others because Jesus is also present in them. Jesus lives within and among us. A true belief in this statement will help us savor the glory of God in the aroma of a fresh scent, the sweet taste of ripe fruit, the sight of a pastoral landscape, the company of a furry friend or the song of a bird in the tree. With John Henry Newman all can pray:

> Dear Jesus, help us to spread your fragrance everywhere we go. Flood our souls with your spirit and life. Penetrate and possess our whole being, so utterly, that our lives may only be a radiance of yours. Shine through us, and be so in us, that every soul we come in contact with may feel your presence in our soul. Let them look up and see no longer us, but only Jesus. Stay with us, and then we shall begin to shine as you shine; so to shine as to be a light to others. The light, O Jesus, will be all from you, none of it will be ours. It will be you shining on others through us. Let us thus praise you in the way you love best by shining on those around us. Let us preach you without preaching, not by words but by our example, by the catching force, the sympathetic influence of what we do, the evident fullness of the love our hearts bear to you. Amen.[3]

There is no time that equals time in Eucharistic Adoration. It is so very precious. Thoughts must fit this occasion. It is best to keep the mind in the present rather than in the past or future. On the grand scale, paying attention to what one is doing now makes daily life easier. Eucharistic adoration is not a time for engaging in idle talk, looking around, daydreaming, thinking of what brought an individual here or what one plans to do afterward. These are all distractions. Failure to concentrate on where we are and what we are doing can lead to brooding about unpleasant things, anticipating negative

---

3. See "Prayer by John Henry Newman," at BeliefNet.com.

results and wondering what others are thinking or saying. Without proper discipline, our thoughts can easily and too frequently be taken over by our imagination.

Holy adoration unfolds into holy living. In the sacred stillness of the church unexpected inspiring thoughts may come to mind: words for a letter that needs to be written, a solution to a long standing problem, a forgotten task that needs attention, a person one must contact, a way to settle an altercation. When our minds are clear and our gaze on Jesus, sometimes, out of the blue, we can sift true from false information, or weigh the pros and cons of a situation more clearly. Quiet times with Jesus help us to live the reality of returning goodwill for ill, love for hatred, and kindness for violence. Visits to the Blessed Sacrament help us to live with care, attention and accountability.

Love of Jesus Inflame Us

Basil Hume, in *The Mystery of the Incarnation*, wrote:

> It is a wonderful practice just to sit or kneel in the presence of the Blessed Sacrament, and in a marvelous way a kind of "presence" begins to reveal itself to us. . . . We need just to be with Christ and to pray. Some may be as Peter, James and John when Our Lord was transfigured on Mount Tabor, hearts full of admiration and joy. But your mood might be quite different, more at ease to be with him, as he was in the Garden of Gethsemane, bringing your pain, suffering and anxieties. Whatever your mood, whatever your concerns, you can in his presence enjoy being with him on Mount Tabor, or suffer with him in Gethsemane. Your mood may be in between those two, a mixture of both. But just being with him, allowing your thoughts and affections to unfurl in prayer in his presence, this will allow those concerns of mind and heart to be blessed and sanctified by him.

If a Catholic is spiritually dry as a sun bleached bone or bereft of any consolation, Jesus is still there. An individual just sits in his presence. One may have nothing to say, but she knows he is there and his mercy is like a soft, refreshing, spring shower. This is faith. Love doesn't need to be a happy experience because faith transcends mere 'good feelings.' To love him even when the heart seems as cold as ice is to sit before him in poverty and helplessness. Ground zero at Eucharistic adoration is emptiness waiting with a mustard seed of faith. Faith deepens as one walks through the dark valleys. Each person receives his cross and watches as it becomes an instrument of salvation. Yes, life has its share of mysterious disappointments, but transformation in Christ fosters a serene outlook. The mystery of trust and hope unites us to the mystery of Christ in the Eucharist. Teresa of Calcutta keeps our gaze in the right direction: "When you look at the Crucifix you understand how much Jesus loved you then. When you look at the Sacred Host you understand how much Jesus loves you now." To gaze at the monstrance will bring about a greater understanding of how love makes pain bearable and, with grace, transforms pain into the joy of sacrifice. It is easier to trust in God if one looks beyond perplexing situations. These situations will eventually be a means of sanctification for humankind. Jesus did not come to explain or end suffering. He sanctifies it by his presence.

A Spiritual Bouquet

Meditation before the Eucharist often inspires consideration of the afterlife. "All who die in God's grace and friendship, but still imperfectly purified, are indeed assured of their eternal salvation; but after death they undergo purification, so as to achieve the holiness necessary to enter the joy of heaven" (*CCC* 1030). A good practice is to include praying for the souls in purgatory. The need for this type of prayer is great. Imagine how many souls are in purgatory! Now imagine how many souls have no one on this earth to pray for them! The second book of Macabees is a reminder: "It is a holy and wholesome thought to pray for the dead so they may be loosed from sin." Catherine of Genoa, who had sound reflections on purgatory, wrote: "The greatest suffering of the souls in purgatory . . . is their awareness that something in them displeases God, that they have deliberately gone against his great goodness." It is very important to pray for souls, especially for the souls who have no family or friends to pray for them.

> O Gentlest Heart of Jesus
> Ever present in the Blessed Sacrament,
> Ever consumed with burning love
> For the poor souls in Purgatory,
> Have mercy on them.
> Especially souls who have no one
> to pray for them.

Everyday Holiness

> Be not severe in thy judgment
> But let some drops of thy precious blood
> Fall upon souls, and do thou O merciful Savior
> Send thy angels to conduct them
> To the everlasting hills of light and peace
> When their purgation
> draws to a close.
> Amen

Someone like Jim could be found among those who knelt in front of the Eucharistic Lord in almost any parish adoration chapel. He was quiet, kind and faithful. His old blue pick-up truck could find its way to the chapel on auto pilot. Jim died a month ago and was finally able to see his Lord face to face. There must have been an instant recognition when Jim's earthly journey came to an end, a joyful union with Jesus and reunion with his loved ones indeed.

Jim was so quiet and humble that few knew much about him, other than he spent regular time at the chapel. A few years ago, Jim lost his beloved wife, his companion of many years. He had many children and grandchildren, but as much as they loved him and he loved them, they could never replace her. But he, our Eucharistic Lord, did. Not in the same way, of course, but as his confidant, as his consoler, as his anchor in the world. Often when Jim spoke about his wife, his "best friend" as he called her, his eyes would fill with tears. However, he did not question God's wisdom, he accepted God's will and went to the adoration chapel day in and day out. In heaven Jim won't be too busy to remember the people at his Nativity parish, and others who need his prayers. It is not uncommon for those in the adoration chapel to think about dear ones who have gone home. In the quiet of the chapel, heaven seems more precious than anything here on earth.

Eucharistic adoration also is an excellent place to offer prayers of reparation to God for the sacrileges against Jesus' Heart and the sins of humanity. Reparation is a humble effort to compensate for the sins of humanity through prayer and penance. We make amends, in other words we strive to repair the damage done by sin. During a person's sacred time with Jesus, she pleads for God's mercy and prays for the sanctification of the Church and world. In the Act of Reparation to the Sacred Heart of Jesus we pray, "How great is the love which you have poured out upon the world.... Kneeling before you we wish to atone for the indifference and the slights which pierce you to the heart. . . . We promise faithfully that by your grace we shall make reparation for our own sins and for those of others by a strong faith, by holy living, and by obedience to the law of the gospel."

Eucharistic adoration is the best possible place to count one's blessings. For seasoned adorers, chants of supplication decrease and songs of thanksgiving increase. To frequently thank God for his goodness is a well-founded habit to cultivate. Gratitude from our heart is a treasure in Jesus' Heart. As time passes, to regularly thank God for his help becomes more beautiful. A litany of things we are thankful for each day can be a real spiritual lift.

The Blessed Sacrament roots humanity in a love that flowers in service. Christ is the primary example for service to others. His love transforms the worst of sins and redeems the world. Peter Eymard noted, "Until we have a passionate love for our Lord in the Most Blessed Sacrament we shall accomplish nothing." Adoration times are the power source that fuels imitating Jesus by good example. We strive to be unwritten gospels leaving the imprint of God's love all around. Living the virtues, offering encouragement and support, trying to stay positive and seeing possibility over reality are not simple practices. A person must look past negative current realities by channeling energy into activities that change things for the better. To infuse graces received from Eucharistic adoration into society is to bring sacred mystery to modern technology, wisdom to scientific knowledge and reverence to people and places. To serve as Eucharist is to be blessed, broken, handed out and to settle for nothing less than holiness.

Jesus Is Everything

> I imagine that I walk into a church at night for adoration of the Blessed Sacrament. The candles on the altar are the only source of light. I rest my eyes upon the host that stands out clear and white against the darkness. The host is like a magnet, for it draws my eyes and being toward itself as to the center. Most of my life I focus on the outer surface, but here I gaze into the very heart of things, the center of my being and of the world. As I keep looking at the host a silence falls upon me. All thinking quiets down and fades away. The silence of that host seems to seep into my body and from there it spreads throughout the church, so everything inside me and around me is stilled. Then as I look the host begins to send out rays of light that enter me and I am grateful, for I know that they will flood my mind,

and my unconscious, cleansing me from all that is self centered and perverse and grasping and afraid. And while the darkness of the church is undisturbed the darkness in my heart is put to flight and all of me is made transparent. The rays now bring with them a holy energy that soaks into my body and fortifies my spirit to face up to the challenges of life. And with their energy a fire spreads all over me to purify my heart of hatred, bitterness, resentment and to give me power to love. So I avidly expose my heart to this life producing sun that shines out at the center of the dark and silent church.[4]

Eucharistic adoration is a source of hope when work is overwhelming. God is the refuge, the rock of ages, the river of life for humankind. Teresa of Calcutta shares a refreshing thought: "When the Sisters are exhausted up to their eyes in work; when all seems to go awry, they spend an hour in prayer before the Blessed Sacrament. This practice has never failed to bear fruit: they experience peace and strength." Time with the Blessed Sacrament puts the brakes on those who run in busy circles. Doing too many good things can prevent a person from responding to the love of God. Slowing down helps us to discern more clearly what is superficial or self-seeking. A slower journey causes the fading of egocentric concerns and enlightens the soul's transformation through Jesus' love.

When captivated by the awesomeness of God, silence replaces words and mercy replaces indifference. Graces in daily life are accepted through listening more attentively and responding more faithfully. Christians reveal who they are by the way they respond to grace. Life is holy in its ordinariness, simplicity and identity in Christ. In Sister Faustina's *Divine Mercy Prayer Book* it says,

> Not only are we to receive and adore the Eucharist, we must live the Eucharist. We are to let the rays of mercy from the monstrance pass through us and go out through all the world. We are to be icons of mercy, radiating love and mercy to others. There is no greater way to energize ourselves to this task than by spending time in the Presence of the Source of Love and Mercy: Our Lord in the Most Holy Eucharist. This is seen in the example given by one saintly priest: "If we were to sit for one hour a few feet away from a radioactive element, how much would that change effect us? The Lord is infinitely more powerful than this and if we go to him seeking grace and mercy, how much more can we hope to be changed?"

---

4. Anthony de Mello, SJ, *Wellsprings*, 62–63.

Silent pauses in adoration are pauses in God's loving embrace. Time spent with Jesus in the Blessed Sacrament revitalizes the spiritual life because here we are in the best of company. Interior silence helps to give full attention to him who is all good. Quiet prayer creates room for God to work. In silent prayer one does nothing and is quite content with watching Jesus. Silence sustains an alert awareness to the transforming value of love. Visits with Jesus are supernaturally refreshing and invigorating. One can truly unwind in the peace that emanates from the presence of Christ. A person is at ease in spite of being weary, perplexed or overwhelmed. God's goodness makes life's difficult aspects easier to accept. Sitting in a still environment with Jesus reaps astonishing graces. Grace reveals what a sublime blessing it is to sit in Jesus' presence and let his love enfold us.

Mother Teresa's Invitation

> I make a Holy Hour each day in the presence of Jesus in the Blessed Sacrament. All my sisters of the Missionaries of Charity make a daily Holy Hour as well, because we find that through our daily Holy Hour our love for Jesus becomes more intimate, our love for each other more understanding, and our love for the poor more compassionate. Our Holy Hour is our daily family prayer where we get together and pray the Rosary before the exposed Blessed Sacrament the first half hour, and the second half hour we pray in silence. Our adoration has doubled the number of our vocations. In 1963, we were making a weekly Holy Hour together, but it was not until 1973, when we began our daily Holy Hour, that our community started to grow and blossom.... That is why I encourage you to make your Holy Hour through Mary, the cause of our joy, and you may discover that no where on earth are you more welcomed, no where on earth are you more loved, than by Jesus, living and truly present in the Most Blessed Sacrament. The time you spend with Jesus in the Blessed Sacrament is the best time that you will spend on earth. Each moment that you spend with Jesus will deepen your union with him and make you soul everlastingly more glorious and beautiful in heaven, and will help bring about an everlasting peace on earth.[5]

---

5. See "Message from Mother Teresa," at EucharisticAdoration.com.

Eucharistia: Holy Communion

IN HIS BOOK *CATHOLICISM: A Journey to the Heart of the Faith*, Bishop Robert Barron concludes his chapter entitled "Word Made Flesh, True Bread of Heaven" with the following paragraph:

> In his meditations on the story of the visit of the Magi, Archbishop Fulton Sheen indicated that the three kings, having traversed a great distance, having withstood opposition from King Herod, having found the baby, having opened their treasures for him, and finally, "having been warned in a dream not to return to Herod, they departed for their country by another way." (Mt 2:12) "Of course they did," Sheen concluded, "for no one comes to Christ and goes back the same way he came!" The liturgy is the privileged communion with the Lord; it is the source and summit of the Christian life. And therefore those who participate in it never leave unchanged; they never go back the same way they came. (194)

In the early church, the words of Jesus, "I am the bread of life," was a true and practical conviction. Early church members led a life of love that was formed around this statement. They received the body of the Lord as bread for each day and this was a constant pledge of that love. It guided and inspired their entire lives. A pagan author wrote: "They are readily recognized by their love for one another." The foundation and source of this love was the bread of Life which they received with great joy.

It is most astounding that God the infinite one, disappears under the appearance of bread and becomes God the humble one, for all humanity. The Dominican, Thomas Aquinas, noted that there would be no real sacrifice or no real communion without the Real Presence. God became man to offer himself on Calvary and continues to offer himself at the sacrifice of the Mass. He became man to give himself to his disciples at the Last Supper and continues to give himself to us in holy communion. He became man to live in the flesh in Palestine, and continues to live now on earth as the same Jesus who died, rose from the dead and is seated at the right hand of the Father. Nothing in human experience is like the Mass. It is utterly unique.

> Let all mortal flesh keep silent,
> And with fear and trembling stand;
> Ponder nothing earthly minded,
> For with blessing in his hand
> Christ our God to earth descendeth,
> Our full homage to demand.
>
> King of kings, yet born of Mary,
> As of old on earth he stood,
> Lord of lords in human venture,
> In the body and the blood
> He will give to all the faithful
> His own self for heavenly food.
>
> ~Liturgy of St. James

The Greatest Treasure

Peter Julian Eymard said: "The Eucharist is the work of a measureless love that has at its service an infinite power, the omnipotence of God." This is what makes the Mass the most beautiful and wondrous aspect of life. No words can adequately explain why or how. The boundaries of time and space disappear. This greatest mystery of our faith is, in fact, our essential reality as Catholics.

The Mass is the greatest prayer and the greatest action on earth. It is more than a collection of words or a memorized ritual. The sanctuary, especially around the altar, is filled with heavenly powers that come to honor him who is present upon the altar. The Mass connects us, the Church militant, with the Church triumphant and the Church suffering. We praise God with the angels and saints in heaven and pray for the souls in purgatory. In the words of John Paul II: "United with the angels and saints of the heavenly Church, let us adore the most holy sacrament of the Eucharist. Prostrate, we adore this great mystery that contains God's new and definitive covenant with humankind in Christ."

The Mass is a reminder that it is good to dwell on communion with the saints. No person stands alone. Everyone is united to the saints in heaven, for they are our brothers and sisters in Christ. Saints are remembered at Mass and are asked to intercede for us. It is comforting and consoling to know that they praise God with us, and intervene for all people on earth who request their intercession. We are one Church gathered together in the communion of the Saints. In the mystical body, the actions and the virtues of good people, contribute to the salvation of all through the communion of the saints. Theodore McCarrick, an American Cardinal, wrote:

> If we truly understood the wonder of the Eucharist, we would never miss Mass on the days when the Church asks us to be present. We go so many miles at so much inconvenience to attend a concert or a meeting or a theater presentation. And yet the greatness of actors and singers and musicians who have ever lived are insignificant when we compare them to the living God. The moments of drama which can be portrayed on stage are elements of lives which do not touch us directly. The drama of the cross which is re-presented and re-enacted in the drama of the Mass touches us to the core of our being because it is through this awesome sacrifice of Jesus that we are saved, that we have a chance at heaven and happiness, that we are given grace to live our lives in light.[1]

Indeed, the Mass is the lifeline of the world, the most powerful expression of love, and the highest means to help others. Nothing can equal the transformation of the bread and wine into his body and blood and the representation of Jesus' sacrifice on Calvary. Augustine helps us to understand this: "Recognize in the bread that same body which hung on the Cross, and in the cup, the same blood which flowed from his side."

Most Profound of Mysteries

This divine sacrifice brings us the holiest of all sacraments: the fullness of the Eucharistic mystery that is Jesus Christ. The Eucharist is the very heart of the Catholic Church. It contains Christ himself and is the principle means by which Christ mysteriously unites the faithful to himself in one body. Through Christ, whose hands still bear the wounds of this world, we join with the priest in offering Christ's body and blood to God the Father. Christ's body, blood, soul and divinity are then received as a priceless gift

---

1. Discourse 228 B, 2.

EUCHARISTIA: HOLY COMMUNION

to us in holy communion. During Mass the saints in heaven worship with us and the souls in purgatory are dearly remembered by us. The Mass is a great, mystic circle of love.

What Jesus did at the Last Supper is a historical fact. Jesus gave his apostles the power to do what he had done. They in turn passed their powers on to their successors so that the privilege of receiving holy communion is available today. Changing bread and wine into Jesus' body and blood is a mystery beyond human understanding and far too magnificent for anyone to completely grasp. No one can adequately explain the Eucharist. An individual must beware of idle curiosity into the reality of Jesus' presence in holy communion. We cannot allow the Eucharist to be something less than what it should be.

The Celebration of the Eucharist is both sacrifice and celebration. It is the source of life and center of love for every Catholic. In the fire of his Eucharistic love, Jesus warms the coldness in our hearts. In the heat of his Eucharistic love, Jesus nourishes us so we can grow in sanctity and be of good service to others. In the flames of his Eucharistic love, Jesus enkindles our love for him anew and keeps faith burning bright in our hearts. Thomas Aquinas wrote a prayer on which to meditate for a lifetime: "O Sacred Banquet in which Christ becomes our food, the memory of his passion is celebrated, the soul is filled with grace, and a pledge of future glory is given to us. O God in this wonderful sacrament, you have left us a memorial of your passion. Help us we beg you, so to reverence the sacred mysteries of your body and blood that we may constantly feel in our lives the effects of your redemption who live and reign forever. Amen."

Indeed, the Mass is the greatest of mysteries, the center of life, the axis of life and the epitome of love around which the Church and world revolves. The consecration is the most solemn action on this earth. The risen Son of the living God becomes present through the words of the priest. The ordinary bread that temporarily nourishes becomes the bread of angels that infinitely nourishes. In the words of the *Catechism of the Catholic Church*: "By the consecration the transubstantiation of the bread and wine into the body and blood of Christ is brought about. Under the consecrated species of bread and wine Christ himself, living and glorious, is present in a true, real, and substantial manner: his body and his blood, with his soul and his divinity" (1413). Who can adequately describe what happens around the altar at this time? It is so far beyond the beyond. This sacramental extension of the incarnation across space and time is the way Jesus continues to abide with his Church. In words from the Angelus, "And the word was made flesh, and dwelt among us." And indeed, he still dwells among us.

> I saw the Sun at midnight, rising red,
> Deep hued yet glowing, heavy with the stain
> Of blood-compassion, and I saw It gain
> Swiftly in size and growing til It spread
> Over the stars; the heavens bowed their head
> As from Its heart slow dripped a crimson rain,
> Then a great tremor shook It, as of pain—
> The night fell, moaning, as It hung there dead.
>
> O Sun, O Christ, O bleeding Heart of flame!
> Thou giv'st thine agony as our life's worth,
> And mak'st it infinite, lest we have dearth
> Of nights wherewith to call upon thy name;
> Thou pawnest heaven as a pledge for earth,
> And for our glory sufferest all shame.
>
> ~Joseph Mary Plunkett

No Greater Love

If people are receptive to the graces given when receiving Jesus in holy communion, their spiritual vision changes to better reflect the light of Christ. Yes, all humans are made in God's image however, they must grow in his likeness. In communion we receive nourishment from Jesus' mercy and love, but we must take that mercy and love and infuse it into our immediate surroundings. Communion infuses Jesus' love into every aspect of our existence. This infusion helps us be affirmed in his love and live by his teachings. The love of God the Father became incarnate in God the Son. God the Son comes to humanity in the form of bread and wine which is his body and blood. Christ in the Eucharist abides in humankind. It is up to humanity to live holy lives so others may know him.

"Abide in me. It is the meaning of the Eucharist," said Elizabeth of the Trinity. What an unparalleled privilege it is to have the Eucharist in our churches. Receiving Christ the Lord, the bread of life, is a call of love that continues to beckon and transform the Church. This great mystery of faith

Eucharistia: Holy Communion

is what is most authentic in this world. The resurrected Christ, the infinite, omnipotent God humbles himself to become present in the form of the most basic of food, bread. Within the Mass, Jesus' glorified body, blood, soul and divinity are with his Church as public worship, social gathering, hearing and teaching of the Living Word, adoration, praise, gift, banquet, sacrifice, and thanksgiving. First and foremost, the Mass is a great mystery where we are drawn into the unseen, intangible world and into the life of the Triune God. Indeed, Jesus abides in his Church.

"Communion with the body and blood of Christ increases the communicant's union with the Lord, forgives his venial sins, and preserves him from grave sins. Since receiving this sacrament strengthens the bonds of charity between the communicant and Christ, it also reinforces the unity of the Church as the mystical body of Christ" (*CCC* 1416).

The more a person receives the Eucharist, the more he will be able to resist temptation and decrease his evil inclinations. He is made wiser and stronger regarding the deceits and temptations of the devil. Interior lights help him to reclaim the virtues and the beauty lost by sin. He withdraws from what is evil and focuses on what is good. Holy communion, worthily received, imparts strength greater than one's own. Jesus provides the strength to do what is best. Immediately after receiving the Eucharist, it is a good practice to place our concerns, hopes and dreams in Jesus' Heart. He is especially in our heart at this time and through this practice, the desires of our heart are in his.

> O Eternal Father,
> Give us this day our daily bread;
> Give us the stillness of heart that will
> Enable us to know you,
> The courage and strength to love your will
> When your will is hard for us,
> The sympathy to watch with you
> And share the cross with you
> To the healing of the nations,
> And the love that alone can save us
> And make us live.
> Amen
>
> ~Gerald Vann, OP

Growing in holiness is like opening sacred gifts. Through holy communion, the deepest expression of Jesus' goodness and love, we grow in human goodness and love. A person is spiritually cleansed, refreshed and revitalized. After lovingly receiving Jesus' body and blood, we ponder the words "Come to me, all who labor and are burdened and I will refresh you," and understand them at a deeper level. They were said for us now and for our future. Hope springs anew. Jesus is always loyal and his tender compassion will last throughout our lives. These words stay in the heart and we take refuge in them when times are tough.

A True Story

Archbishop Fulton Sheen was very inspired by the following story. When the communists took over China, they imprisoned a priest in his rectory near his church. After they locked him up, the communists went into the church. In the sanctuary, they broke into the tabernacle, pulled out the ciborium and threw it on the floor. The consecrated hosts spilled out. There were thirty-two hosts scattered on the sanctuary floor.

When the communists left, they did not notice, or did not pay attention to, an eleven-year-old Chinese girl praying at the back of the church. She saw everything that happened. That night the girl came back and quietly, because she did not want to wake the guard, went into the church. She remained in prayer for an hour, because she wanted to make an act of love in reparation for the act of hate shown to Jesus in the Eucharist. After her prayer, she went into the sanctuary, knelt down, bent over and with her tongue received Jesus in holy communion. (People did not receive the sacred host in their hands at this time.)

She quietly prayed and received communion each night for thirty-two nights. On the thirty-second night, after she had consumed the last host, she accidentally made a noise that woke the sleeping guard. He ran after her, caught her, and beat her to death with the butt of his rifle. Her martyrdom was witnessed by the grief-stricken parish priest still held captive in his rectory.

This frail young girl gave an extraordinary witness to the real presence of Jesus in the Eucharist. She showed true courage and authentic zeal. She exemplified how faith can overcome fear and how love for Jesus in the Eucharist transcends life itself. Just as the sun in the sky is the natural source of energy, so Jesus in the Eucharist is the supernatural source of grace and love.

Eucharistia: Holy Communion

We move toward Jesus in many ways: in prayer, the sacraments, sacramentals, rites and rituals, and sacred reading. However, the most excellent way is through holy communion. He dwells within in an indescribable way which is most perplexing to worldly people. This food of immortality creates a very special union and is the most perfect expression of his boundless love for us. Through frequent holy communion we are blessed by grace to lead a God fearing life and reach the heavenly homeland. In *Story of Soul*, Therese of Lisieux says, "Our Lord does not come down from heaven everyday to lie in a golden ciborium. He comes to find another heaven, which is infinitely dearer to him—the heaven of our souls, created in his image, the living temples of the adorable Trinity."

In mysterious ways Jesus' body and blood, under the appearance of bread and wine, acts upon souls like food and drink act upon bodies. Jesus does not come near a physical body, but he comes into the soul. According to Leo the Great, who died in 461 and left many letters and writings of great historical value: "For the effect of our sharing in the body and blood of Christ is to change us into what we receive." If a Catholic shares in Jesus' life, he or she must live by Jesus' way. The passing wonders of the world are nothing compared to the grace of holy communion. If Catholics receive communion with a firm faith, steady hope and tender love, their souls will gain strength, endurance and resilience.

We must be reverent when we receive communion. How might this be done? Catholics try to avoid receiving communion in an idle, routine, mechanical way by concentrating on who they are receiving. Catholics genuflect when they enter and leave the church and incline their heads before receiving communion. When Catholics walk in the communion line they neither slouch, nor saunter down the aisle with arms dangling at the side. They are going to meet the King of Kings so they walk in dignity, with hands folded and body straight. Their attire reflects the respect they have for the Lord of Lords by modest, clean and dignified dress. Unkempt, untidy leisure wear is inappropriate for church. When receiving holy communion, Cyril of Jerusalem wrote: "In approaching, therefore, come not with thy wrists extended, or thy fingers spread; but make thy left hand a throne for the right, as for that which is to receive a King. And having hollowed thy palm, receive the body of Christ, saying over it, Amen. So then after having carefully hallowed thine eyes by the touch of the holy body, partake of it; giving heed lest thou lose any portion thereof; for whatever thou losest, is evidently a loss to thee as it were from one of thine own members. For tell me, if any one gave thee grains of gold, wouldest thou not hold them with all carefulness, being on thy guard against losing any of them, and suffering loss? Wilt thou not then much more carefully keep watch, that not a crumb fall from thee of what is more precious than gold and precious stones?"

Imelda's Reflection

I would like to share my way of putting myself into the Mass instead of just attending it. I began attending daily Mass years ago to thank the Lord for a favor received. I had intended it to be just for the summer, but by the end of summer I was hooked. As time went on, I grew more and more to appreciate the sublime wonder that it is. In catechism classes, we were taught that the Eucharist is the commemoration of the passion and death of Jesus. But how is the raising of the body and blood of Christ a memorial to death? It came to me in the separate raising of the body and then the blood, for when blood is separated from the body, death occurs. Because we believe that this is the body and blood of Christ, then that which we are witnessing is the death of Christ. Also, in catechism we were encouraged by the sisters to unite our own sufferings to that of Christ. When the priest puts that drop of water into the wine, I offer to Jesus what at that time is causing me grief. Just as that drop of water becomes thoroughly one with the wine, so does my suffering become one with the suffering of Christ. When Jesus' passion and death are offered to God the Father, I can feel sure that my own suffering is in them. When I receive Jesus in holy communion, I receive him as the Jesus who triumphed over his own suffering and death and he shares that triumph with me. I can then feel confident that I have the strength and grace to triumph over my own problems.

To Love and to Serve

Reverence should be in season at all times and in all places. It doesn't stop when one exits a church, but continues as a sign of love toward all people. Reverence waters the seeds of goodness. Being open to the graces in frequent communion is like absorbing rays from a warm sun. As flowers of reverent goodness burst into bloom, a higher quality of life bursts forth. The desire for wanting to be good changes to being good and then doing good for others. On Holy Thursday Jesus put on an apron and washed the feet of his apostles. Followers of Jesus must do the same. Hands that are

EUCHARISTIA: HOLY COMMUNION

reverently folded when receiving holy communion also tie on the apron of service. Each Christ centered person is a little sign of Jesus' infinite goodness. Her good works are usually simple and done without notice. Eucharistic grace urges everyone to move back and forth, from worship to service. Jesus is with us and consequently we become more awake to opportunities of respectful service. Relying less on natural inclinations and more on the teachings of Jesus, an individual finds his judgments and choices to be more Christ like. Frequent reception of communion uncovers more areas of service in one's home and fosters doing daily tasks with love and reverence. To act and speak politely is to treat people and things with care and respect. Respect during communion resonates in courtesy shown to others. The greatest spiritual union, holy communion, sanctifies the many small acts of love in daily existence. If communion should become a dull routine, taken for granted, or a comfortable gratification, one needs to think of the billions of people who live their whole lives without the spiritual benefits that are accessible to Catholics. Communion is the greatest of gifts and through it we are grateful for the smallest of gifts. How an individual values the reception of communion in church is measured by the quality of one's conduct in the world.

It is lovely to see fragments of the attributes of Jesus in others. At times to see them is a challenge, but not a difficult one. He is in the kindness of a fellow parishioner, the care of a health professional, the concern of a neighbor, in people who serve in organizations that help the needy, from a local clinic to an international organization. People respectfully serve others in a local Senior Center or in a foreign mission. Christians who wear aprons of service, take people grocery shopping, provide companionship to the lonely, comfort for the dying and help for those who mourn. Some are social justice advocates for the downtrodden. Others have gifts that inspire people to greater love, support others when they are down, or cheer for their achievements. A Christian looks around and easily sees the body of Christ in action. In a moment of desperation someone appears from nowhere to help. As the sun sets and the evening shades are drawn one asks: "How did I meet Jesus today?" Like the disciples on the road to Emmaus, we often do not recognize Jesus at the job site, market, bank or home. He comes around in all shapes, colors, sizes and cultures. When we see him where we haven't seen him before, we smile and say thank you.

The elderly woman slowly gets out of her car. It has been her habit to attend daily early Mass and she had done so for many years. However, the years are catching up as she feels the diminishment of age. She moves slowly to the church door. The pain and unsteady gait causes her to be more attentive to her walking. She does not want to fall and uses a cane to steady herself. Pain is like an old familiar friend these days, yet she has to admit that sometimes she gets perturbed with her friend. She enters the church and goes to her accustomed place. She mostly sits through Mass. At communion she shuffles carefully up the aisle. After the Mass she remains still, resting her head on her hands seemingly absorbed in quiet prayer. The priest gazes at the woman in the stillness after Mass. He ponders how she was active in so many ministries in the past, but is now engaged in her most central ministry. He muses that the woman's love of prayer brings strength to this church. She is important to the parish. This woman and others like her, although not involved in busy parish activities, are the backbone of the parish because of their unwavering prayer.

After communion we sit quietly with minds still and let Christ speak to us in wordless communion. The more receptive we are to God's love, the more we are transformed by that love. As we commune with the Divine, we begin to see life the way Jesus sees it. Our way of thinking changes. Eucharist is the best opportunity for enabling us to be good friends of Jesus.

We should never take communion for granted for "Having passed from this world to the Father, Christ gives us in the Eucharist the pledge of glory with him. Participation in the Holy Sacrifice identifies us with his Heart, sustains our strength along the pilgrimage of this life, makes us long for eternal life, and unites us even now to the Church in heaven, the Blessed Virgin Mary, and all the saints" (*CCC* 1419).

> I know a secret key which never fails
> to open the gates of divine mercy;
> I know a river which will carry us
> into the promised land;
> I know a palm tree which will shelter us
> from the burning heat of our earthly exile;
> I know a spring whose refreshing waters slake
> our thirst in the desert of this life;
> I know a star which will guide us
> as the pillar of cloud guided Israel,
> across the sandy ocean of our existence
> to the end of the journey.

Eucharistia: Holy Communion

I know a dew which God sheds from heaven
and which must sustain us for the remainder
of the road we have to travel.
I know a tree whose wood can sweeten
the bitter waters which are our
portion to drink here below,
and make them give us a foretaste
of the heavenly Canaan;
I know a victim whose sacrifice ascends
in an odor of sweetness to
the God of Abraham.

And this secret key,
this river,
this palm tree,
this star,
this heavenly dew,
this holocaust,
is the Eucharist.

~Hermann Cohen
(Father Augustine of the Blessed Sacrament, OCD)[2]

---

2. See Tierney, *Story of Hermann Cohen*, 3.

Mystery: The Ineffability of God

AN ONGOING THEME IN life and in faith is mystery. The older we get the more mystery impacts us. Living with the mysteries of our Catholic faith is neither for sissies nor for those who blindly follow traditions and customs. It is all or nothing. Either we face God who is incomprehensible, or we run away. Speech vanishes when Christians contemplate the mystery of God. There is no prattle. They stand mute before God. Indeed, mystery lies beyond us for it is too rich for our comprehension. Basil Hume explains:

> The meaning of things and their purpose is, in part, now hidden, but it will in the end become clear. The choice is between the mystery and the absurd. To embrace the mystery is to discover the real. It is to walk towards the light, to glimpse the morning star, to catch sight from time to time, of what is truly real. It is no more than a flicker of light through the cloud of unknowing, a fitful ray of light that is a messenger from the sun which is hidden from your gaze. You see the light but not the sun. When you set yourself to look more closely, you will begin to see some sense in the darkness that surrounds you. Your eyes will begin to pick out the shape of things and persons around you. You will begin to see in them the presence of the One who gives them meaning and purpose, and that is he who is the explanation of them all.[1]

Every time a mystery is somewhat understood it gives rise to the exploration of new mysteries. Mysteries generate wonder at the reality of God all around us. Jesus said: "I have come that you may have life and have it more abundantly" (John 10:10). An abundant life is one grounded in holiness. Only through holiness, can a person become complete and more fully a person of God. Holiness is the way people become more alive in the Lord which verifies the great goodness of God. We deeply consider the words

---

1. Hume, *Mystery of Love*, 1.

of John Paul II: "When you wonder about the mystery of yourself, look to Christ who gives you the meaning of life. When you wonder what it means to be a mature person, look to Christ who is the fullness of humanity. Because actions speak louder than words, you are called to proclaim by the conduct of your daily lives that you really do believe that Jesus is the Lord."

No person on this earth has the ability to know completely the One who gives meaning to all. God is the greatest mystery. Some things are known about him. God, and his attributes, are only partially comprehensible because of his vast mystery. Each person also shares the mystery factor. Do we really understand a loved one? Do we totally understand ourselves?

God's Majesty

In 1913, at his home in New Jersey on a cold winter's afternoon, a poet wrote the first two lines of a new poem in his notebook. These two lines were followed by what was to become one of the most inspiring verses in America. Unfortunately, Joyce Kilmer did not live to see just how famous his poem became. He enlisted during World War I and was a member of the Fighting 69th Infantry Regiment. At the age of thirty-one, he was killed in action in France.

> I think that I shall never see
> A poem as lovely as a tree.
>
> A tree whose hungry mouth is prest
> Against the earth's sweet flowing breast,
>
> A tree that looks at God all day,
> And lifts her leafy arms to pray;
>
> A tree that may in Summer wear
> A nest of robins in her hair;
>
> Upon whose bosom snow has lain;
> Who intimately lives with rain.
>
> Poems are made by fools like me,
> But only God can make a tree.

The mystery of God's creative power is so obvious in nature. Even though a person may know the scientific reasons for natural phenomena, such as leaf positions to sun and shade, they do not detract from mystery. An individual is still in awe of the grandeur of God when he looks at the fiery colors in fall foliage, the migrating birds, cloud formations, the turning of tides, sprouting seeds and, most of all, life developing within a woman's womb. Christians understand through facts, but are wise through mystery. According to Thomas à Kempis: "If the works of God were such as might be easily comprehended by reason, they could not be called wonderful or unspeakable."

An unknown poet wrote: "We cannot speak of God, he is beyond compare. And so we can adore him best by silent prayer." This bit of verse drifts around in the mind when, in quiet and stillness, an individual contemplates a snowy field in early morn, the sun on ripened grain, stars glittering at night or a sleeping newborn baby. Many inspiring things in life are mysterious, and are most appreciated in silence because words fail to describe them. From the space above us, to the sea below us, from the telescopic to the microscopic, life seems veiled in mystery. A divine mist adds enchantment, and sometimes aggravation, when seeking God. We want to know. We think we know. And then we realize how much we do not know. Thomas Aquinas was a luminous Dominican and doctor of the Church. His writings were characterized by brilliant thought and lucid language. They filled twenty hefty tomes. One day near the end of his life, when Thomas was celebrating Mass, a great change came over him. This change caused him to cease writing or dictating. He could do no more because such things were revealed to him that everything he had written seemed to be straw. No single person, or group of people, has eyes, ears or mind keen enough to understand the fullness of God. A Greek Orthodox theologian teaches us: "We see that it is not the task of Christianity to provide easy answers to every question, but to make us progressively aware of a mystery. God is not so much the object of our knowledge as the case of our wonder."

A component of mystery is wonder. A sense of wonder keeps a person's heart young. A child is absorbed in awe as he watches a spider spinning a web or ants at work. The mysteries in wonder are deep and rich and do not need fine thoughts or descriptive words. Because nature reflects the creativity of God, it is reverent and sacramental. A Christian needs only to gaze at lilies in the field, trees in a forest, quiet lakes or rugged mountains to see them as signs of grace.

Mystery: The Ineffability of God

Indeed, the world is full of incomprehensible wonder. God's creative energy is bright, bold and powerful. Despite man's indifference to, and spoiling of, God's creative works, Nature will continue to replenish and refresh herself through the renewing grace of the Holy Spirit. This is quite evident when one sees a flower growing through a crack in a sidewalk. In the words of an old hymn: "Summer and winter and springtime and harvest, sun, moon and stars in their courses above, join with all nature in manifold witness, to thy great faithfulness, mercy and love." Man will only realize his capacity for fullness when he sees himself as part of the order of God's world. Although humankind has not always treated God's creation well, God continues to reveal himself in the world. He speaks through his renewable creation. The Holy Spirit embraces the world like a mother embracing her child.

> The world is charged with the grandeur of God
> It will flame out, like shining from shook foil;
> It gathers to a greatness, like the ooze of oil
> Crushed. Why do men then now not reck his rod?
> Generations have trod, have trod, have trod;
> And all is seared with trade, bleared, smeared with toil;
> And wears man's smudge and shares man's smell;
> The soil is bare now, nor can foot feel, being shod.
>
> And for all this, nature is never spent;
> There lives the dearest freshness deep down things;
> And though the last lights off the black West went
> Oh, morning, and the brown brink eastward springs—
> Because the Holy Ghost over the bent
> World broods with warm breast
> And with ah! Bright wings.
>
> ~Gerard Manley Hopkins

Incredible Beauty

John Scott wrote: "Our God makes possible the beauty of precious stones and carved ivory, of sunsets behind mountain ranges, and sunlight after storms at sea, the thrill of glorious music, the calm satisfaction of graceful architecture, flowers at their crest, waterfalls at their laciest, the warmth of charity, the reassurance of friendship, the happiness of youth, all these God makes possible. Our God is a beautiful God. Beauty exists because he is its boundless source. Artists create beauty because he, the great artist, not only gave the urge to follow his creative example, but filled the world with beauty in many lines and colors."[2]

Every person has a unique makeup. Therefore, every person is differently affected by the various aspects of beauty. Beauty reflects the multifaceted elegance of God. A person perceives beauty through the senses, intellect and the soul. In various ways and in different degrees, beauty is manifest in nature, art, music, literature, worship, prayer and most of all in a human being. On earth, the fullness of beauty is deep holiness within an individual. Holy beauty includes moral beauty such as the beauty of humility, chastity, patience and other virtues. Although profound, holy beauty is rarely appreciated by society. Holiness is beauty at its most mysterious form because the one who is all beauty, Christ, is its source. With holy beauty, an individual becomes more alive to, and more delighted by the unfathomable mystery of the Triune God.

With grace, each person is an ongoing expression of God's beauty with a unique combination of colors and design. Watching Christ's love mysteriously unfold in someone's life is a beautiful experience. Love for God strengthens the love one has for others. This is evident when unrealistic expectations of others are dropped. No one person can meet all the needs of another. Every human person is a mystery to be learned slowly, reverently, with care and with prayer. We can never know another person completely, but we can love him or her completely. Love given without expectations is hard to do, but it is a more authentic way to love. Teresa of Avila said that love does not consist in the extent of one's own happiness, but in the firmness of one's determination to please God in everything and to advance the glory of his son.

Ultimate Exquisiteness

Any attempt to describe what makes something or someone beautiful usually ends in mystery. Beauty is magnificently and wondrously baffling.

---

2. Quoted from "The Living Spirit," a regular column of about five quotes that was in *The Tablet*, an international weekly review published in London (date unknown). John Scott (1730–1783) was an English poet.

Mystery: The Ineffability of God

Observe the splendor of a baby in the womb. The baby's growth and development is the most rapid, the most eventful and the most intricate during these nine months than at any other time in the baby's life Early development of a baby in the womb is immensely complex. Each baby's life is unique and precious. At conception the fertilized egg, smaller than a grain of salt, contains all the genetic information for every detail of the newly created life and is unlike that of any other human being. Jerome Lejeune, a medical doctor, doctor of science, and professor of fundamental genetics in Paris, who discovered the genetic cause of Down syndrome, said that the first cell, the fertilized egg, is "the most specialized cell under the sun." He continues: "Each of us has a very precise starting moment which is the time at which the whole necessary and sufficient genetic information is gathered inside one cell, the fertilized egg, and this is the moment of fertilization. There is not the slightest doubt about that and we know that this information is written on a kind of ribbon which we call the DNA."

Although the growth rate of each baby will vary, there are general developmental patterns that are truly awesome. During the first month, the baby is about one fourth of an inch long; the heart is beating and pumping blood through the body. The eyes, ears, mouth, nose, kidneys and liver have begun to develop. The baby is ten thousand times larger than at the time he or she was as a fertilized egg at conception.

In the second month, the baby is about one inch long. The skeleton is in the process of forming, the hands and feet begin to move. The mouth, ears and nose are taking shape. Brain waves can be measured and the baby responds to touch (comfort and pain). Every organ is present and functioning. The kidneys produce urine. The brain coordinates movement. At this stage, the baby is called a "fetus" which is Latin for "young one" or "offspring."

It the third month the baby is over two inches long, has unique fingerprints with fingernails and toenails. It opens and closes the mouth, sucks the thumb, moves and kicks. The brain grows rapidly. Each minute it produces almost 250,000 new neurons.[3] The baby will bend its fingers around an object placed in the palm, and the hands, feet, arms, legs, and most of the body look clearly human. All organs and systems are functioning.

During the fourth month the six-inch, seven-ounce baby squints, puckers up brow, swallows and urinates, smiles and frowns, makes a fist and hears mother's voice and heartbeat. The baby's movements are felt by

---

3. Focus on the Family, "The First Nine Months," 11.

the mother. The umbilical cord transports twenty-five quarts of fluid per day and completes a round trip of fluids every thirty seconds.

In the fifth month, the baby is about ten inches long, weighs about a pound, with eyelashes and hair beginning to grow. Sleeping habits appear, a slammed door provokes activity. The baby responds to sounds in frequencies too high or low for adults to hear.

During the sixth month, oil and sweat glands are functioning. The baby's delicate skin is protected by a special ointment (vernix).

In the seventh month, the baby is fourteen inches long and weighs about two and a half pounds. Mother's voice is heard and recognized. The baby's hands grip strongly and the four senses of vision, hearing, taste and touch are used.

During the remaining months the baby will nearly triple in weight. In the eighth month, the skin begins to thicken and a layer of fat is stored underneath for insulation and nourishment. The baby is ready for birth toward the end of the ninth month. Of the forty-five generations of cell divisions before adulthood, forty-one have taken place in the womb. Only four more will come, during the rest of childhood and before adolescence. In developmental terms, we spend 90 percent of our lives in the womb.[4]

Life is a precious and mysterious gift, from conception to natural death. It deserves protection and respect. Modern culture, with its vast technical resources and medical advancements, often misses the beautiful mystery of creation. It is too consumed with its own intellect to accept what it cannot fully understand. Christians have a serious obligation to promote and defend human life and religious freedom. Sound Christians are needed to hammer the sharp nails of moral truth into the wood of public policy by persuasive, rational, courteous and intelligent argument. "Lord Jesus, once you spoke to men upon the mountain, in the plain. O help us listen now, as then, and wonder at your words again. We all have secret fears to face, our minds and motives to amend. We seek your truth, we need your grace, our living Lord and present friend. The gospel speaks, and we receive your light, your love, your own command. O help us live what we believe in daily work of heart and hand."[5]

---

4. Human Life Alliance of Minnesota, "She's a Child Not a Choice," advertising supplement (St. Paul, 1995), 3. Other sources: pamphlets from Human Life International (Gaithersburg, MD); Heritage House (Snowflake, AZ); and Physicians for Life, www.physiciansforlife.org (Cullman, AL).

5. H. C. A. Gaunt, in *Liturgy of the Hours*, 2:1121.

Mystery: The Ineffability of God

Enlightenment

Like the sun beams its dappled rays through ever-moving clouds, so does moments of mystery penetrate the routine of our daily lives. Life is a journey in a land of mystery. The effects of mystery range from playful to sober. We experience mystery not only in prayer and in suffering, but also in unexpected circumstances and surprising behaviors. Henri Amiel observed: "We are hemmed around with mystery, and the greatest mysteries are contained in what we see and do every day."

On a day-by-day journey it is no surprise that, at times, an individual is at loose ends. Life seems more than one can bear. It is said that the darkest hour is just before dawn. There is grace for just that darkest hour. In the nights of great tragedies, there is also grace. Tornadoes, floods, fires, and terrorist attacks can be the source of spontaneous charity, unity, and harmony. People go beyond themselves to help others. They become other-directed, without concern for themselves. Heroic acts and great kindnesses happen during national tragedies. Why does it take a tragedy? It is strange how these events bring to mind basic questions of life: Why am I here? Where am I going? How will I be remembered? Why did my neighbor die and I survive? How God brings good out of tragedies is one of the most profound mysteries pondered by the believer.

How a person responds to mystery defines what kind of person he or she is. The mystery in negative things, such as hate, violence and injustice challenge the fortresses of love, goodness and truth. Endurance is shored up by grace. However, grace is a gift that must be received, opened and accepted. To live out the mystery of grace is to react to a negative situation in a positive way. Rain cancels a picnic in the park, but the people enjoy looking at the rain while having an indoor picnic. This is a constructive interpretation of a negative experience. When she was almost fourteen years old, Therese of Lisieux was surprised by the mystery of grace. She wrote in *Story of a Soul*:

> It was December 25, 1886, that I received the grace of leaving my childhood, in a word, the grace of my conversion. We had come back from Midnight Mass where I had the happiness of receiving the strong and powerful God. Upon arriving at Les Buissonnets, I used to love to take my shoes from the chimney corner and examine the presents in them; this old custom had given us so much joy in our youth that Celine wanted to continue treating me as a baby since I was the youngest in the family. Papa had always loved to see my happiness and listen to my cries of delight as I drew each surprise

from the "magic shoes," and my dear King's gaiety increased my own happiness very much. However, Jesus' desired to show me that I was to give up the defects of my childhood and its innocent pleasures. He permitted Papa, tired out after the Midnight Mass, to experience annoyance when seeing my shoes at the fireplace, and that he speak those words which pierced my heart: "Well, fortunately, this will be the last year!" I was going upstairs, at the time, to remove my hat, and Celine, knowing how sensitive I was and seeing the tears already glistening in my eyes, wanted to cry too, for she loved me very much and understood my grief. She said, "Oh Therese, don't go downstairs; it would cause you too much grief to look at your slippers right now!" But Therese was no longer the same; Jesus had changed her heart! Forcing back my tears, I descended the stairs rapidly; controlling the poundings of my heart, I took my slippers and placed them in front of Papa, and withdrew all the objects joyfully. I had the happy appearance of a queen. Having regained his own cheerfulness, Papa was laughing; Celine believed it was all a dream! Fortunately, it was a sweet reality. Therese had discovered once again the strength of soul which she had lost at the age of four and a half, and she was to preserve it forever![6]

This story shows how a positive response to grace makes a person a better follower of Jesus. Instead of crying, Therese smiled. She also smiled when sisters interrupted her as she was writing her autobiography while sitting in her wheelchair in the cloister garden. The sisters would come up to her and chat. Therese was irritated by this because she wanted to concentrate on her work. However, she chose to greet the sisters kindly instead of voicing her aggravation at them. How can we develop Therese's good habit? At the end of each day we can spend a few minutes thinking of negative responses we made during the day. Is there a habitual pattern? Do we complain about our supervisor to the same coworker at the same place during a same time period? Who, what, and when are necessary when identifying a negative trait. Then perhaps, with the aid of grace, we can change negative complaints to positive compliments. This takes determination and drive. It is said that the best players on a basketball team are the shortest people. Why? Because they practice, practice and practice every day. So is it with holiness. Natural talents or a high intelligence are not imperative in striving for holiness. However, determination and drive are most necessary. Negative events in life are easier to bear when a person does not swim against the tides of pessimism, but floats in the currents of God's mercy.

6. Therese of Lisieux, *Story of a Soul*, 98.

If an individual floats in the water of Divine Providence, he sees how humanity is bound together by shared fatigue, suffering, but most of all, love. Goodness begets goodness. The choice is ours. We can curse an agonizing condition or we can do something constructive to alleviate it. We can add to the negative in a negative situation or offer hopeful solutions to change it. We continue to serve others without knowing what the next day will bring. We move ahead in spite of pain and fear. Someone once said, "We have our brush and colors. We paint paradise and in we go. We paint hell and in we go." Painting heaven or hell is our choice and we cannot blame anyone for what we create. In the words of a short poem: "In you is hell's abyss, in you is heaven's grace. What you elect and want, you have in any place." We may not understand the mysteries that deliver all our circumstances in life, but we can trust that God has allowed them for our enrichment.

Mysterium Fidei

Mysterium Fidei, or the mystery of faith, holds the mysterious threads of life together. It is the primary factor in maintaining a positive demeanor and keeping commitments. Long term fidelity is not easy. However, we strive to be faithful to the tenets of our Christian way of life no matter how hard that life may be. For example, we pray when it is the last thing we want to do. We live and work with people that we no longer find interesting, attractive or compatible. We stick with it when we tire of our work, or have a wearing schedule. We keep going even when we do not know where our road of life is leading. We are encouraged by the revered spiritual leader Metropolitan Anthony Bloom:

> Every encounter is an encounter in God and in his sight. We are sent to everyone we meet on our way, either to give or to receive, sometimes even without knowing it. Sometimes we experience the wonder of giving what we did not possess, sometimes we have to pay with our own blood for what we give. We must also know how to receive. We must be able to encounter our neighbor, to look at him, hear him, keep silence, pay attention, be able to love and to respond wholeheartedly to what is offered, whether it be bitterness or joy, sad or wonderful. We should be completely open and like putty in God's hands. The things that happen in our life, accepted

as God's gifts, will thus give us an opportunity to be continually creative, doing the work of a Christian.[7]

Although it is hard to see Jesus in trials, annoyances and suffering, he can be found if one looks beyond outward appearance and with the mystery of faith. Jesus takes on many disguises. Patience helps make it possible to see Jesus in humanity's distressing disguises. If we are struggling with a relationship, it can be a precious opportunity to offer to Jesus. The difficult relationship would be a way to enlarge our hearts by embracing the person as he or she is instead of how we want him or her to be. Christians find peace in taking people as they are and waste no time wishing they were otherwise. Patience helps to cultivate the habit of thinking kindly about others. Those who rub us the wrong way may be the sandpaper that will make us saints. Patience is a serene grace. Problems patiently endured work toward a person's spiritual good. We learn to endure suffering and evil for long periods of time because patience enhances the ability to carry burdens with love. With composure and self control, we tolerate suffering for the love of God and the love of others.

It is true that patience does not seem natural. Often there is nothing more illusive than staying with something for a long period of time. Waiting is not popular. Yet, it keeps an individual on the right track when experiencing difficult circumstances and fuels determination in the face of delay. Patience helps to avoid negative actions when annoyed or angry. We try to hold our tongue when unkind or snappy words come to mind because once a harsh word is said, it cannot be taken back. Patience nurtures self control whether under short-term strain or long-term difficulties.

To make haste slowly are wise words to live by. We are assisted by Gregory the Great: "In times of uncertainty, wait. Always, if you have any doubt, wait. Do not force yourself into any action. If you have a restraint in your spirit, wait until all is clear, and do not go against it. Hold to patience in your hearts, my friends, and put it into action when the situation calls for it. Don't let any abusive word from your neighbor stir up hatred in you, and don't allow any loss of things that pass away to upset you. If you are steadfast in fearing the loss of those things that last forever, you will never take seriously the loss of those that pass away. If you keep your eyes fixed on the glory of our eternal recompense, you will not resent a temporal injury. You must bear with those who oppose you but also love those you bear with. Seek an eternal reward in return for your temporal losses."

7. Bloom, *Courage to Pray*, 33.

Mystery: The Ineffability of God

Because God dwells in the heart so mysteriously, faith in him is deeper, richer and more challenging. Faith is the surest refuge and the greatest strength even though its paradoxes are baffling. We cannot be filled with God until we are empty of ourselves. We cannot find our life unless we lose it. We cannot have all unless we have nothing. We are nothing so God can use us for anything. We cannot experience the white heat of God's love unless we experience the dark cold of suffering. We cannot forgive others until we eliminate evil from ourselves. We become strong in weakness and wise through failures. Who can explain these things? John Henry Newman wrote:

> Religion has its very life in what are paradoxes and contradictions in the eye of reason. It is a seeming inconsistency how we can pray for Christ's coming, yet wish time to 'work out our salvation' and 'make our calling and election sure.' It was a seeming contradiction how good men were to desire his first coming, yet were unable to abide it; how the apostles feared, yet rejoiced after his resurrection. And so it is a paradox how the Christian should in all things be sorrowful yet always rejoicing, and dying yet living, and having nothing yet possessing all things. Such seeming contradictions arise from the want of depth in our minds to muster the whole truth. We have not eyes keen enough to follow out the lines of God's providence and will, which meet at length though at first sight they seem parallel.[8]

A Christian ponders the mystery of God in the simplest and most universal of all human activities, prayer. Prayer is a source for revitalization, and an utter enigma. It mysteriously leads us in our nothingness to him who is all. Silent prayer is more profound than wordy prayer. We find deep contentment in sitting quietly next to God and observe our longing for him converge with his longing for us. Spiritual peace remains even though prayer doesn't bring what we want or answers our questions. The need to figure God out gives way to a settling into his mystery.

Mystery removes Christians from conventional paths. One understands by not understanding. One feels a void inside, yet faith has never been more substantial. An individual arrives at a place to find he has already been there. As people's lives become simpler, their souls have the opportunity to become more profound.

And Christians learn. They are helpless without Jesus. Mary of Nazareth experienced many things that she could ponder but not, understand.

---

8. Newman, *Parochial and Plain Sermons*.

Like her, Christians strive to live peacefully with the element of mystery. Mary stood by the cross and shared the helplessness of Jesus. She did not walk away. Joseph, a smart and capable man, could not have understood the mystery of Mary's pregnancy, nor the urgent prompting to move his vulnerable family to Egypt. But he trusted and responded as a man of faith, and in doing so played a pivotal role in the story of our salvation. The history of our faith is rich with stories of faithful men and women who not only accepted the mysteries God delivered into their lives, but embraced them with holy abandon.

At times there are no answers. Jesus' crucifixion shows that the more love an individual brings into a situation the more vulnerable she becomes. Even though a Christian deeply feels the pain of another, he cannot eliminate the other's Calvary. Those who succeed in loving must go through pain and many small deaths. A death may be the inability to help except through prayer, the service of the heart.

Many times in our lives, we stand alone at the foot of the cross in prayer. If we feel lonely or sad, we take courage because in God's mysterious ways, loneliness can change to solitude and sadness can change to wonder. At this point, we discover our oneness with the Triune God. We are very conscious of his dwelling within us and are at peace with this mystery. As we deepen in our reverence for mystery, and the confusion in life calms and we can live in relative peace with the unknown, the unexplained and the unresolved elements of life. In time mystery becomes sweet to us, as long as we trust in God, place our concerns in his hands, and walk in hope.

> God moves in a mysterious way,
> His wonders to perform;
> He plants his footsteps in the sea,
> And rides upon the storm.
>
> Deep in unfathomable mines
> Of never failing skill,
> He treasures up his bright designs,
> And works his sovereign will.
>
> Ye fearful saints, fresh courage take,
> The clouds ye so much dread
> Are big with mercy, and shall break

Mystery: The Ineffability of God

In blessings on thy head.

Judge not the Lord by feeble sense,
But trust him for his grace;
Behind a frowning providence
He hides a smiling face.

His purposes will ripen fast,
Unfolding every hour:
The bud may have a bitter taste,
But sweet will be the flower.

Blind belief is sure to err,
And scan his works in vain;
God is his own interpreter,
And he will make it plain.

~William Cowper

Gratitude: A Hymn from the Heart

WHEN JESUS IS THE center of our lives, gratefulness is always present in the depths of our hearts. John Baillie explains: "A true Christian is a man who never for a moment forgets what God has done for him in Christ, and whose whole comportment and whole activity have their root in the sentiment of gratitude." Gratitude is an echo of love in the heart. These echoes remind Christians to appreciate all their gifts and warn them to safeguard the door of their hearts so that grateful love remains a primary virtue. A sentinel, in the form of a sturdy conscience, keeps good things in the heart and protects it from evil intrusions. Bitterness, cynicism, indifference, discouragement and other negative factors pull people into self absorption. Reconciliation, trust, support, courage and related positive traits push people out of themselves and nurture a welcoming and grateful demeanor. Many times the forces of good and evil are in heavy combat. Every sin is an act of ingratitude, a gift misused. Each time a Christian says thank you to God, the forces of evil diminish. Prayer and grace help good to prevail over evil. Pastor Martin Rinckart, served in a German town named Eilenburg that became a refuge for military and political fugitives during the Thirty Years War. Eilenburg became overcrowded with refugees who were victims of famine, and victims of the Black Plague epidemic that arrived in 1637. Pastor Rinckart buried two of the town's four pastors on the same day and the third one fled to a healthier climate. As the sole remaining pastor, Rinckart conducted as many as forty to fifty funeral services a day, totaling to about 4,480 funerals. While living in this town that was dominated by death, Pastor Rinckart is best known for writing this hymn:

> Now thank we all our God
> With heart and hand and voices,
> Who wondrous things has done,

In whom this world rejoices;
Who, from our mother's arms,
Hath blessed us on our way
With countless gifts of love,
And still is ours today.

O may this bounteous God
Through all our life be near us,
With ever joyful hearts
And blessed peace to cheer us;
Preserve us in his grace,
And guide us when perplexed,
And free us from all ills
In this world and the next.

~Martin Rinckart
(1586–1649)

Bearing Suffering Gracefully

Often, even the most difficult things can help us in one way or another. John of Avila advises: "One act of thanksgiving when things go wrong with us is worth a thousand thanks when things are agreeable to our inclinations." To be only thankful for the things that are agreeable to us does injustice to the word "gratitude." Someone said if we bear our burdens cheerfully, we are halfway to becoming saints. There is much suffering in life. Alphonsus Liguori offers wisdom: "If we have any natural defect, either in mind or body, let us not grieve and be sorry for ourselves. Who is there that ever receives a gift and tries to make bargains about it? Let us, then, return thanks for what he has bestowed on us. Who can tell whether, if we had had a larger share of ability or stronger health, we would have possessed them to our destruction?" Gratitude helps Christians recognize that what they have is enough. When difficulties disrupt our comfortable patterns, with patience and trust, the chaos will settle into order and confusion into clarity. Gratitude brings peace into the present and establishes a vision of hope for the future.

How can we bear our suffering cheerfully? It takes prayer. Christians should not fear telling God why their lives are hard, senseless or difficult.

God welcomes people to talk to him with simple and trustful words that come from the center of the heart. God is always inviting Christians to holiness, to sanctify those moments that are difficult. Some circumstances tempt us to become bitter or resentful, even toward God. Examples could be a minor irritant, or a major disease, the loss of someone or something, the fear of such a loss, or an unexpected trauma. An individual could be the scapegoat for someone's aggression or hurt. When these things happen the first thing to do is to practice forgiveness. Sometimes we must begin by asking God for the desire to forgive. A Christian must pardon before she is pardoned. Do I need to pardon, or ask for pardon, from a neighbor, God or myself?

When a Christian feels angry or discouraged because things are not going his way, he can react or reflect. Lack of reflection keeps him at a superficial level. Although certain situations are hard to understand, reflection helps a person pay attention to what has happened and leads to discoveries hidden beneath the surface. Sometimes things are not what they appear to be. Even in the bitterest misfortune, Christians know by faith that God sees what has happened, and will strengthen the soul through it. We can thank him for that good work, even though we may not understand what it is. Pardon may not change our mood immediately, but if it is sincere, it lessens or even neutralizes the sting of the memory, even the memory of something that happened a few days ago. The Angel Gabriel said to Mary, "The Lord is with you." We believe the Lord is with us as well. He is at the center of our hearts in times of light and darkness. We can imagine holding his hand as we walk forward in good and bad times. We keep asking God to be with us and seek to be more responsive to his presence again and again.

'Tis a Gift

God, in his infinite goodness, gives each of us unique gifts. It is up to us to develop these gifts, and, with grace, to use them well. By using them well, we bring fragments of God's goodness to others, thereby sharing the joy of faith. A result of gratitude is satisfaction with our gifts. There may be more peace, true joy and love in a person whose life is seemingly monotonous, uneducated and deprived than in a person who is brilliant, successful and admired. A Christian does not need to be rich, clever, pretty or handsome. Thoughtful advice is given by Dietrich Bonhoeffer: "In ordinary life we hardly realize that we receive a great deal more than we give, and that it is only with gratitude that life becomes rich. It is very easy to overestimate the importance of our own achievements in comparison with what we owe others." It is easier to ruminate about what we lack than to dwell on what we possess.

Looking at someone else's life from the outside, and seeing it as much more rewarding then our own, is not an accurate assessment. Gratitude concerning our own circumstances releases the hold of an overactive imagination and grounds a person in what is real. Complaining about what we don't have opposes gratitude. Many possessions weigh a person down. Too much time is spent acquiring them, paying for them, cleaning and maintaining them and ultimately disposing of them. All this takes lots of energy. When does a person say "that's enough"? If an individual can live with "enough" he will worry less about what is unnecessary. The words of an old Shaker hymn come to mind: "'Tis a gift to be simple, 'Tis a gift to be free, 'Tis a gift to come down where we ought to be. And when we come down to a place just right, it will be in the valley of love and delight." It is a beautiful gift to live simply.

Christians pray, "Give us this day our daily bread." Remembering yesterday's needs were met enables an individual to trust in God for the needs of tomorrow. Indeed, the accomplished person is someone who needs the least and leaves this world better than he or she found it.

> We thank you then, dear Father,
> For all things bright and good.
> The seedtime and the harvest,
> Our life, our health, our food.
> And all that we can offer,
> Your boundless love imparts.
> The gifts to you most pleasing
> Are humble, thankful hearts.
>
> ~M. Claudius

Gratitude flowed from the pen of Wilferd Peterson:

> The art of thanksgiving is thanksgiving. It is gratitude in action. It is applying Albert Schweitzer's philosophy: "In gratitude for your own good fortune you must render in return some sacrifice of your life for other life." It is thanking God for the gift of life by living it triumphantly. It is thanking God for your talents and abilities by accepting them as obligations to be invested for the common

good. It is thanking God for all that men and women have done for you by doing things for others. It is thanking God for opportunities by accepting them as a challenge to achievement. It is thanking God for happiness by striving to make others happy. It is thanking God for beauty by helping to make the world more beautiful. It is thanking God for inspiration by trying to be an inspiration for others. It is thanking God for health and strength by the care and reverence you show your body. It is thanking God for the creative ideas that enrich life by adding your own creative contributions to human progress. It is thanking God for each new day by living it to the fullest. It is thanking God by giving hands, arms, legs and voice to your thankful spirit. It is adding to your prayers of thanksgiving acts of thanksgiving.[1]

The Divine Plan

God's divine plan offers great challenges today. Media ads nourish greed and covetousness among consumers. The latest technical gadgets on TV seem to be more attractive than the gadgets already in our home. Soon after we buy something new, the sparkle around it fades. It holds our attention for a while then ends up in a drawer. The lure of novelty is always present. Excess is a great temptation. Over consumption keeps the credit card companies in business. Being a follower of Jesus is like rowing up a river against the current. However, there is grace in those oars.

It is true that living gratefully takes grit. The secular world's strong emphasis on materialism and consumerism prevent a person from enjoying and being grateful for what he has, and drives him to want more and more. This leads to a perpetual feeling of dissatisfaction and unhappiness with what he has and who he is. The me centered orientation of today's society can lead a person to think he is entitled to everything. As a result, he thinks he has the right to possess without giving anything in return and without giving thanks for what he is given. Gratitude counteracts these popular beliefs. Christians must be always on the alert. People's egos can wear attractive disguises and can be present in concealed ways that erode basic human rights. A hungry ego consumes what should go toward the basic needs of humanity. Christians believe that each person is made in the image of God, and he or she deserves dignity and respect. Human rights

1. Peterson, *Art of Living*, 1961.

come from God. They cannot be interpreted without him. Civil leaders, who define human rights without God's laws, and without respect for the sanctity of life, can end up with atrocities that destroy life. Humanity must live by God's plan or else it is doomed to destruction.

Jesus reveals God's plan to us. It is replete with blessings in many forms. Christians enjoy blessings everyday, but forget to give thanks for most of them because they are so common or so routine. A quiet heartfelt thank you whenever a blessing comes along is a lovely custom. Gratitude is minute attention to the variety of God's gifts in the particulars of one's day. It is consciousness living the reality that God really loves and cares for the least and smallest of us. Gratitude is in full bloom when there is a radical trust in God. Christians should strive to be grateful for everything in their lives.

Virginia is a lovely, soft-spoken woman of eighty-two years. She lives alone in a small senior citizen's apartment in southern California. Her husband passed away six years ago. She smiles when she talks about the happy times during the many years of marriage to her husband. Virginia does not indulge in self-pity. Because her vision is not what it used to be, Virginia had to surrender her driver's license. She sees the loss of her car as a gain because of the money she saves by not having to pay for gas, car insurance and maintenance. She gets her exercise by walking to the store and brings the purchases home in her little cart. If she can't walk anymore she will get a scooter. Her thinking is very positive and she always looks at the bright side of situations. She has some memory loss, but has learned to write things down and is thankful for her organizational skills. She is a retired grammar school teacher who was loved and respected by her students. Always appreciating the value of an education, she volunteers at a local library and helps children learn to read. When looking at photographs taken of her she does not make disparaging remarks about herself, not even in jest. Virginia believes that life is good and she does her best. She does not fear the future and looks forward to heaven. Several years ago, she cut out and saved an article that was in her archdiocesan newspaper. The article inspired her to take better care of her furnishings and other possessions, and to make sure they go to a woman's shelter when she passed on.

The article reads:

> When I was a novice in our Oblate novitiate, our novice master tried to impress upon us the meaning of religious poverty by making us write two Latin words, ad usum, inside of every book that

was given us for our own use. Literally the words translate into "for use." The idea was that, although a book was given to you for your personal use, you were never to think that you actually owned it. Real ownership lay elsewhere. You were only a steward of someone else's property. This idea was then extended to everything else that you were given for your personal use—your clothes, your sports equipment, things you received from your family, and even your toiletries and toothbrush. You got to use them, but they were not really yours. You had them ad usum.

One of the young men in that novitiate eventually left our community and went on to become a medical doctor. He remains a close friend and one day while I was in his office I picked up one of his medical textbooks. I opened the cover and there were the words, ad usum. When I asked him about why he did this, he made a comment to this effect: "Even though I no longer belong to a religious order, and no longer have the vow of poverty, I still like to live by the principle that our novice master taught us: In the end, we don't really own anything. These books aren't really my own even though I've paid for them. They're mine to use, temporarily. Nothing really belongs to anybody and I try not to forget that."

What ultimately under girds all spirituality, all morality and all authentic human relationships is the unalterable truth that everything comes to us as gift so that nothing can ever be owned as ours by right.[2]

Everything ultimately comes from God and is given to us on loan. Everyone should have the charming gift of knowing a few people like Virginia. She lived the words of the wise and gentle bishop, Francis de Sales: "Do not fear what may happen tomorrow. The same loving Father who cares for you today will care for you tomorrow and every day. Either he will shield you from suffering or he will give you unfailing strength to bear it." Anne Frank is another example. When in hiding for two years from the Nazis, Anne noted in her diary that she saw beauty in the world and was grateful for it. Yes, beauty is everywhere and in some sense reflects aspects of God's beauty. Many like Anne teach others how they can love the unlovable and forgive the unforgivable. When Christians reach this level there is authentic belief that Jesus is the way, the truth and the life. If we love the Lord, we must do as he says and remember that he always has our salvation

---

2. Ronald Rolheiser, OMI, "Ad Usum," *The Tidings*, November 21–28, 2008.

in view, no matter what happen to us. Many times things do not go the way we planned. In the words of a Confederate Soldier:

> I asked God for strength, that I might achieve;
> I was made weak, that I may learn humility to obey.
> I asked God for health, that I may do greater things;
> I was given infirmity, that I might do better things.
> I asked for riches, that I may be happy;
> I was given poverty, that I might be wise.
> I asked for power, that I might have the praise of men;
> I was given weakness, that I might feel the need of God.
> I asked for all things, that I might enjoy life;
> I was given life, that I might enjoy all things.
> I got nothing I asked for but everything I hoped for.
> I am, among all men, most richly blessed.

A Grateful Orientation

Expressing gratitude can be a very simple and spontaneous custom that sanctifies time and place. At the close of the day, to thank God for a few specific things that happened during the day is a beautiful habit to formulate. Each week, in a "gratitude journal" we may want to write down names of people, events, challenges met, fears over come, simple gifts or any other area for which we are thankful. Each topic has its own page. A gratitude journal would be good to read when we are feeling discouraged or down hearted. As time goes on, we are more grateful because we can identify more blessings. Gratitude gets easier with practice. Happy moments in life come freely and unexpectedly. To stop and enjoy these moments with a sense of wonder and thanksgiving opens hearts to serendipity and attentiveness. Pondering the good things instead of lamenting about what we do not have or what we cannot do. Smiling and saying "thank you" for everything received, even for things that seem small and unimportant. Taking care of what we have and sharing it with others who have not. Conserving our use of food, water, electricity or other resources. Thanking others with action such as a note, phone call, etc. Responding to questions in letters, email and other media. Changing "a favor for a favor" to a favor given without any expectations of having it returned. Using phrases like "If you would permit me. . ." "Would you be so kind as to. . ." "Excuse me, sir. . ." They are not anachronisms of the past but a refinement of present speech.

Courtesy in the home fosters respect for one another. The way spouses address each other indicate their regard for each other. The words and tones they use will be observed and even repeated by their children. Making a habit of small courtesies, like saying, "I'm sorry, I didn't hear what you said," instead of "Huh?" or using someone's name instead of "Hey" or "I am not amused" instead of "You make me so mad" develops an atmosphere of Christian gentility. Contrary to modern thought, the home is not a place where one can completely relax by saying what one wants or dressing as one pleases. These things do not make for a happy home. A love for and practice of courtesy develops an awakening to the sacred and a deepening reverence to God and for each other.

To have a grateful heart is a beautiful gift. Because it is a sacred responsibility to reflect God in whatever circumstances life brings, Christians serve as sign posts that point to Jesus and his gospel teaching. Verbal gratitude echoes the compassion of God. If a Christian does not express the gratitude she feels in her heart, it is like keeping a wrapped gift instead of giving it to the person for whom it was intended. Christians are the windows through which people see glimpses of the kingdom of God. The more Christians express gratitude for the graces of God, the cleaner their windows will be. Indeed, God sends so many graces. We have seen something quite ordinary for a hundred times and suddenly it is beautiful. We never really considered the great blessing of basking in God's love. Graces sparkle everywhere. In people who see what is not right and try to correct it. In people who do not blame others for their bad choices and forgive easily. In individuals who respectfully listen to opposing views of others without mitigating the essentials of their faith. When we affirm goodness in others, and become a safe harbor for them, the graces of love and gratitude flow freely. If we slide into ungratefulness, we do not use God's gifts as well as they could be used. We must keep our eyes on Jesus in order to use our gifts as best we can. Without Jesus we cannot reach our full humanity and therefore can easily get full of ourselves.

We would rather be filled with God. Gratitude to God for the smallest of graces broadens our view of the workings of grace. Someone once wrote: "The view from the dining area faces north onto a side yard, replete with large oak trees. As I enjoy my morning coffee, squirrels chase each other up and down the trees while the coo of the morning doves and chirps and warbles of the various birds fill the air as they jockey for positions at the bird feeder. The creek burbles along in front of a large, lightly treed pasture. A few clouds dot the bright blue sky and a gentle breeze rustles the light branches. Christ is risen, Alleluia! All is right with the world. The peace is almost palpable and fills me with warmth more penetrating than the coffee. This is indeed God's place. Let us give thanks and be glad."

> O Lord of heaven and earth and sea,
> To thee all praise and glory be;
> How shall we show our love to thee,
> Who givest all?
>
> The golden sunshine, vernal air,
> Sweet flowers and fruit thy love declare,
> When harvests ripen thou art there,
> Who givest all.
>
> For peaceful homes and healthful days,
> For all the blessings earth displays,
> We owe thee thankfulness and praise,
> Who givest all.
>
> Thou didst not spare thine only Son,
> But gav'st him for a world undone,
> And freely with that blessed one,
> Who givest all
>
> Thou giv'st the Spirit's blessed dower,
> Spirit of live and love and power,
> And dost his sevenfold graces shower
> Upon us all.
>
> For souls redeemed, for sins forgiven,
> For means of grace and hopes of heaven,
> Father, all praise to thee be given,
> Who givest all.
>
> ~Christopher Wordsworth

Song Without End

A complete expression of gratitude is both interior and exterior. The internal disposition is a grateful heart that recognizes all gifts received. This is followed by an external expression of words or deeds that acknowledges and gives credit to the giver of a gift. Some type of appreciation is expressed, and when it can be done, some gesture of gratitude is extended for what has been freely given without any obligation from the donor.

As the psalmist says, "It is good to give thanks to the Lord." The ongoing song of the heart is gratitude. How grateful are we for the many good things we receive? Part of gratitude is defining gifts and reflecting on their richness. God offers us so much: There is no one else like me in this world. I am welcome to God's mercy when I sin. I receive grace to do penance for my sins and to resist temptation. I have the Sacrifice of the Mass, sacraments, sacramentals, spiritual friendships . . . the list is endless. If we follow God with everything we do, saying "thank you" to him becomes a frequent, loving response. Indeed, it is impossible to count the many blessings we receive from the providence of God. Therefore, we are ever grateful for the delight and privilege of who we are and what is around us.

Each person has several melodies from which to sing songs of gratitude. This would be an unending finale in the symphony of God's compassion. The discordant notes of self-serving pleasure are avoided. The activities of compassion never dominate, manipulate, control, possess or cause inappropriate dependency. The melodies of gratitude are never finite and always follow an interactive process that involves ordering values and activities in appropriate life sustaining ways. If compassion were the great opera of life, each song would praise God and respect each human being as a child of God.

The habit of gratitude matures us. We look back and see that we were able to help, not hurt; to remedy, not reveal; to elevate, not diminish; to illuminate, not darken. The pastel colors of gratitude are quiet and inconspicuous, finding their way into the artistry of the passing days. In muted shades, joy is given to the down hearted, rest to those who are weary and quiet to those who are too busy. The grace of God helps Christians to be loving, patient, gentle, tender and ever grateful for his gifts. Christians strive to be empathetic in the way Atticus Finch describes in the novel *To Kill a Mockingbird*: "You never really understand a person until you consider things from his point of view. . . . Until you climb into his skin and walk around in it." To immerse oneself in the conditions of humanity is to enter into their pain, brokenness, confusion and anguish. Gratitude is threefold: It is the virtue that makes us aware of the gifts we receive each day. It moves us to respond to these gifts by developing them, using them well and putting them at the service of others. It makes us more appreciative of the generosity of God.

> Jesus, thy boundless love to me,
> No thought can reach, no tongue declare;
> Unite my thankful heart to thee,
> And reign without a rival there!
> Thine wholly, thine alone, I am;
> Be thou alone my constant flame.
>
> John Wesley (trans.)

Bibliography

Allen, Charles. *God's Psychiatry*. Westwood, NJ: Revell, 1958.
———. *The Secret of Abundant Living*. Old Tappan, NJ: Revell, 1980.
Barclay, William. *The King and the Kingdom*. Grand Rapids: Baker, 1980.
Barron, Robert. *Catholicism: A Journey to the Heart of the Faith*. Word on Fire Catholic Ministries. New York: Image, 2011.
Bloom, Anthony. *Courage to Pray*. Mahwah, NJ: Paulist, 1973.
———. *Creative Prayer*. London: Darton, Longman & Todd 1987.
Bonniwell, William R. *The Life of Blessed Margaret of Castello*. Rockford, IL: Tan, 1983.
Casey, Michael. *Strangers to the City: Reflections on the Beliefs and Values of the Rule of St. Benedict*. Brewster, MA: Paraclete, 2005.
Christopher, Kenneth, ed. *A Sampler of Devotional Poems*. Mahwah, NJ: Paulist, 1997.
Ciszek, Walter. *He Leadeth Me*. San Francisco, CA: Ignatuis, 1995.
Commission on the Liturgy and Hymnal. *Service Book and Hymnal*. Minneapolis: Augsburg, 1958.
Dubay, Thomas. *Beauty Coming Alive*. 4 discs. Home Video Series. Irondale, AL: Eternal Word Television Network, 2007.
Engstrom, Ted. *The Making of a Christian Leader*. Grand Rapids: Zondervan, 1978.
Fénelon, François. *Talking with God*. Translated by Hal M. Helms. Brewster, MA: Paraclete, 1997.
Focus on the Family. "The First Nine Months." Pamphlet. Colorado Springs: Focus on the Family, 2008.
Groeschel, Benedict. *The Saints in My Life: My Favorite Spiritual Companions*. Huntington, IN: Our Sunday Visitor, 2011.
———. *Spiritual Passages: The Psychology of Spiritual Development*. New York: Crossroad, 1983.
———. *The Journey toward God*. Ann Arbor, MI: Servant, 2000.
Hartmann, Helen Louise, and Janice Brickey. *Journey of Love: The Way of the Cross through the Eyes of a Mother*. Paterson, NJ: St. Anthony Guild Press, 1960.
Harty, Gabriel. *The Riches of the Rosary*. Dublin: Veritas, 1997.
Hume, Basil. *The Mystery of Love*. Brewster, MA: Paraclete, 2001.
———. *The Mystery of the Incarnation*. Brewster, MA: Paraclete, 2000.
Hutchings, Margaret. *Teddy Bears and How to Make Them*. Mineola, NY: Dover, 1964.
Kelly, William L. *Women before God: Prayers and Thoughts*. Westminster, MD: Newman, 1961.

Bibliography

Kubicki, James. *A Matter of the Heart: Meditations on the Sacred Heart of Jesus and the Consecrated Life.* Libertyville, IL: Institute on Religious Life, 2010.

———. *Rediscovering Devotion to the Sacred Heart of Jesus: A Heart on Fire.* Notre Dame: Ave Maria, 2012.

Lindbergh, Anne Morrow. *Hour of Gold, Hour of Lead.* San Diego: Harcourt, Brace, Jovanovich, 1932.

Liturgy of the Hours. Vol. 2, *Lenten Season–Easter Season.* Prepared by the International Commission on English in the Liturgy. New York: Catholic Book Publishing, 1976.

Liturgy of the Hours. Vol. 3, *Ordinary Time Weeks 1–17.* Prepared by the International Commission on English in the Liturgy. New York: Catholic Book Publishing, 1976.

Louis of Blois. *Spiritual Works of Louis of Blois.* London: Aeterna, 2015.

Maasburg, Leo. *Mother Teresa of Calcutta: A Personal Portrait.* San Francisco: Ignatius, 2011.

Merton, Thomas. *I Have Seen What I Was Looking For: Selected Writings of Thomas Merton.* Edited by M. Basil Pennington. Hyde Park, NY: New City Press, 2005.

———. *The Waters of Siloe.* Garden City, NY: Image, 1962.

Mother Teresa. *Love: A Fruit Always in Season.* Selected and edited by Dorothy Hunt. San Francisco: Ignatius, 1987.

Newman, John Henry. *The Idea of a University.* London: Aeterna, 2009.

———. *Parochial and Plain Sermons.* San Francisco: Ignatius, 1997.

Nyquist, Pat. *Spirit & Life* magazine (Benedictine Sisters of Perpetual Adoration, Tucson, AZ), March/April 2007.

Peterson, Wilferd. *The Art of Living.* New York: Simon & Schuster, 1961.

Pope Gregory I. *Be Friends of God: Spiritual Reading from Gregory the Great.* Cambridge, MA: Cowley, 1990.

Reinhold, H. A., ed. *The Soul Afire: Revelations of the Mystics.* New York: Pantheon, 1944.

Renfree, Harry A. *Beyond the Horizon: Daily Devotions for Seniors.* Edited by Gordon Renfree. Eugene, OR: Wipf & Stock, 2016.

Smith, Herbert F. *Homilies on the Heart of Jesus and the Apostleship of Prayer.* Staten Island, NY: Alba House, 2000.

Stein, Edith. *The Hidden Life.* Washington, DC: ICS, 1992.

———. *Life in a Jewish Family, 1891–1916: An Autobiography.* Washington, DC: ICS, 1984.

Stravinskas, Peter, ed. *Our Sunday Visitor's Catholic Encyclopedia.* Huntington, IN: Our Sunday Visitor, 1991.

Swindoll, Charles R. *Swindoll's Ultimate Book of Illustrations & Quotes.* Nashville: Nelson, 1998.

Therese of Lisieux. *Story of a Soul: The Autobiography of Saint Thérèse of Lisieux.* Translated by John Clarke. Washington, DC: ICS Publications, 1975.

Thomas, à Kempis. *The Imitation of Christ.* Edited by Clare Fitzpatrick. New York: Catholic Book Publishing, 1977.

Teilhard de Chardin, Pierre. *Activation of Energy: Enlightening Reflections on Spiritual Energy.* Orlando: Mariner, 2017.

Tierney, Tadgh. *The Story of Hermann Cohen O.C.D.: From Franz Liszt to John of the Cross.* Oxford: Teresian, n.d.

United States Conference of Catholic Bishops. *Catechism of the Catholic Church.* Libreria Editrice Vaticana. New York: Catholic Book Publishing, 1994.

www.ingramcontent.com/pod-product-compliance
Lightning Source LLC
Chambersburg PA
CBHW050800160426
43192CB00010B/1586